THE DOG'S GUIDE TO FAMOUS OWNERS

The Dog's Guide

o Famous Owners

HELGA DUDMAN

Robson Books

First published in Great Britain in 1997 by Robson Books Ltd, Bolsover House, 5-6 Clipstone Street, London W1P 8LE

British Library Cataloguing in Publication Data
A catalogue record for this title is available from the British Library

ISBN 1 86105 056 9

Printed by The Guernsey Press Company Ltd., Guernsey, Channel Islands

Introduction

You are about to meet an extraordinary and exclusive collection of Very Important Persons. Specially selected for one specific trait and brought together here for the first time, they include some of the most interesting, powerful, creative, scholarly, rich (but also poor) and historically important men and women who ever lived.

The one thing they have in common is their attachment to the dog/dogs in their lives — their Very Important Pooches. This canine connection has hitherto been neglected as a key to VIP character. From now on, it may now be considered as a distinct new academic sub-division, enabling us to meet the great personages of our world through their dogs.

The people who helped make our world are increasingly forgotten in our age, and every day brings us more and more to forget. But it is, for instance, a safe bet that after encountering Frederick the Great in bed with his three greyhounds, you will manage to retain his place in your mind in an unforgettable way.

The famous owners you will find on every page include kings and poets, presidents and scholars, generals and scientists, mistresses and hermits, theatrical stars and philosophers, saints and sinners and Nobel Prize winners. To be sure, not all occupy the very top rank of fame; but every one would add enormously to any gathering. And as to determining Top Dog at any show, when is there always agreement as to who gets the Blue Ribbon? I have followed only one immutable rule: no famous name, however exalted, has been admitted to the pages that follow without his/her dog.

A magnificently varied pack of humans, these Famous Owners lived in different countries and in different eras, and they are as unlike each other as the variety of dogs who shared their lives — as different in looks, in outlooks, in behaviour and in personality, as the Pomeranian is from the Newfoundland, the collie from the poodle. Their relationships to their dogs are also of course all different — for when are love affairs ever alike?

If there is a dog in your life, then you know that you are already in excellent company. As has so often been said, the dog is the most loyal, understanding, useful, versatile, and appealing four-legged companion known to man. All this is so widely known that no further book on the subject of canine virtue is required. (The cat question will be touched on, lightly petted.)

But this is only part of the Best Company consideration. The fact is that, by virtue of your dog you are also in illustrious human company. What is more: you probably never realized it, but because of your canine experience, you (and not your dogless neighbour!) have a ready-made area of conversation with, say, Alexander the Great or Jean Jacques Rousseau — given the initial embarrassment and possible language problems.

As the collection grew — it is admittedly random, and could easily have been ten times as large — it began to take on the nature of a party — a celebration of people and animals who could never otherwise have met, but who, the moment they would arrive with their elegant invitations, would find topics of ever-present interest to discuss.

We might imagine an early English scientist in earnest con-versation with a much earlier Greek poet about the problems of house-training. Or, to begin naming names, Gertrude Stein and Arthur Schopenhauer on the poodle personality . . . Odysseus and his famous loyal hound giving the eye to Barbara Bush and her spaniel, these days even more famous . . . William Randolph Hearst's dachshund, down there with the other dachshunds, eying his co-breed owners (a Norwegian movie star, a German chemist, a Swedish physician, a Victorian poet . . .). And cat-lover Samuel Johnson, who went shopping himself for oysters for his cat Hobbes because he was too embarrassed to ask his housekeeper to make this extravagant purchase. Johnson had this to say about dogs: "I would rather see the portrait of a dog that I know, than all the allegories they can shew me in the world." And here, of course, we learn as much about Dr Johnson's view of life as about his respect for animals.

And as the coats, crowns, and togas of the Very Important People are politely taken at the door and the various leashes hung nearby, the Very Important Pooches, snouts up, would already be eagerly leading their masters to the food. Tea and cakes, whiskey for the owners — greatly appreciated by quite a few of the assorted humans. Neatly presented on the floor, bones and biscuits and, to the astonishment of the guests from ancient Egypt and Greece, kibbled dog food in assorted flavours, surely a high point of modern civilization.

As you have noticed, this is a deceptively educational social event. How many people today remember much about Bismarck? Not to mention Simonides? Or even Byron, or Descartes? But they are well worth retrieving from the past (yes, certainly we have retrievers too), and re-discovering great personalities via their dogs is an excellent way of getting good grades.

Here and there, it must be admitted, you will also find some neurotic and melancholy types among the owners; and as will be seen, there are case histories and theories about the transmittal of tragedy from owner to dog. You will also find an Eternal Triangle here and there. Not in the sense of two excited male dogs panting at a bitch in heat, but rather through some of the problems in human romantic relations in which the dog played the third corner of the triangle. Very interesting.

Of course, there are also owners who were poor during their

lifetimes and achieved only posthumous renown. A few were even not very nice. But they are famous, and that is what human history is all about. As for their dogs, any defects they acquired could have been chalked up to their masters, or to the kind of distressing situation in which we all find ourselves, dogs as well as humans. As James Thurber, the great American humourist and observer of men, women and dogs put it,

If I have any beliefs about immortality, it is that certain dogs I have known will go to heaven, and very, very few persons.

And for a change of pace and to underline the point, Napoleon:

I was walking across the battlefield when suddenly a dog crawled out from under the coat of a dead soldier. He began to howl piteously and to lick the face of his dead master.
I have given orders for battles that resulted in huge casualties without any particular feeling of emotion. But here I felt deeply touched and agitated by the sounds of the dog's anguish.

Can Animals Communicate?

Psychologist Stanley Coren has stated unequivocally that "a dog has never written an opera or a novel," going on to include "designing bridges or exploring cybernetic space" as further projects beyond any dog's capacities. (So when did *you* last write an opera or explore cybernetic space?) Coren also attacks the earlier "behaviouristic" view of animal limitations; for a further discussion of this point, see Monsieur Grat and his owner, René Descartes.

At about the time the Coren book appeared, a best-selling French neurologist, psychiatrist, and psychoanalyst (*sic*) published *How Does my Dog see my Cabinet?* (translated here from the German, a translation from the original French), which assures us that dogs and humans view the world totally differently and warns us against the perils of anthropomorphism. Well, bow wow!

For the moment, I will stick with Harvard biologist (and palaeontologist and science historian) Stephen Jay Gould. Addressing the always timely topic of the chimpanzee's capacity for intellectual communication, he notes: "I am beginning to suspect that we will learn everything we want to know directly from the chimps themselves." And remember when probabilists used to say that, given enough time, paper, and computers, a bunch of chimps would eventually write all of Shakespeare?

But this is a post–modern viewpoint. Dogs and other animals have spoken volumes in literature, especially in children's literature, and in super-modern best sellers. (*See* Millie, written, purportedly, by a dog, and a female at that.) *Black Beauty* comes to mind — the "autobiography of a horse," although the royalties were collected by a woman, Anna Sewell, who published it in 1877. A distinguished contemporary professor reminds us that

One cannot write a sentence in the first person without a momentary suspension of commonplace identity, whether the putative speaker is the Pharaoh of Egypt or a cocker spaniel.

He had in mind Thomas Mann (*see* Bashan) and Virginia Woolf (*see* Flush).

This glamorous canine-VIP-gathering is, as noted, far from comprehensive. Tracking down all eligible invitees would have taken several lifetimes: canine connections are, after all, not computerized, and discoveries are often a matter of luck.

Missing Note

Smart readers may worry about many fine "missing" specimens: the three dachshunds of Somerset Maugham, for instance. Or the Pomeranian who, with a parrot, shared the life of Edward Gibbon and his *Decline and Fall of the Roman Empire*. Or Emily Brontë, on the moors with her beloved dogs Keeper and Flossy, dreaming of *Wuthering Heights*. Or diarist Samuel Pepys arguing in bed with his wife about their dog who "fouled" the house. Or, in very

other times and places, TV star Phil Donahue and his big white Labrador.

The reason for these and other non-appearances is principally lack of space: our dog-party is not *really* in eternity, but only in a finite book. This is why we have included only one of the mythological and cosmological dogs eternally in the heavens, and only fearless "Zodi," the "little dog" constellation of astronomy, is with us, to close this book.

Then too, there are cases when the dog's presence is recorded, and sometimes his breed, but not his individual name. After many (dogged?) attempts to track down names and/or breeds, I decided when necessary to invent names and bestow them on the dog in question, and I made this a useful game by constructing *mnemonic devices*. The beauty of this, as you will see, is that the concept of the mnemonic device has been attributed, probably wrongly, to an early Greek poet who was also profoundly attached to his hound. (*See* Lycas.)

And then there is that wonderful old question, What is Truth? The comforting phrases "scholars disagree" and "dubious historicity" crop up so often in fat research tomes that in due course I stopped worrying about who would check up on what.

The much-viewed and well-known dogs in paintings, films, and in literature make only a few appearances here. There are just too many of them, and what might be said about them and their owners did not always strike me as fascinating.

One of the most recent best-selling dogs to write his autobiography is Boy (same name, but not to be confused with Prince Ruprecht's). This Boy is a charming shaggy mongrel who lives in Provence with best-selling author Peter Mayle, who has superbly communicated Boy's adventures and views on life. Boy even has a chapter on "The Art of Communication." He is briskly clear about his feelings about fancier dogs: poodles, for instance ("we all know what little toadies *they* are"), and cocker spaniels who, when faced with a problem, can think of nothing better than to lie helplessly on their back. *A Dog's Life* is, in short, even better than a trip to Provence.

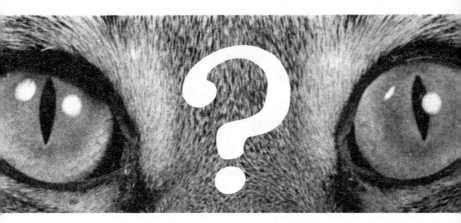

The Cat Question

Some VIP owners had cats as well as dogs. Some didn't. Some people, as we all know, don't like either: and these, as Munthe said (*see* Gorm), are only to be pitied. There is no end of famous owners of cats, among them Mohammed (according to legend), Martin Luther, Lenin, Victor Hugo, Baudelaire, Mark Twain, Doris Duke, James Mason, President Bill Clinton. Try to extract some psychological theory out of this listing.

Cat lover Mark Twain had this to say about dogs: "If you pick up a starving dog and make him prosperous, he will not bite you. This is the principal difference between a dog and a man." But of course all of Twain's many statements about animals had basically to do with his view of mankind.

Much has been written — mostly unprovable — as to what makes a dog person as opposed to a cat person. Some (mostly cat lovers) maintain that dog lovers want someone they can boss around and can educate. Cat lovers feel they (the lovers) are a finer breed because they enjoy the "uneducability" of cats, their grace and beauty, their existence in, as it were, another world.

"Artists love cats, soldiers love dogs," says animal researcher Desmond Morris, in what seems a much disproved rule. But cats do abound in paintings; attributed to Leonardo da Vinci is the saying that "Even the smallest kitten is a work of art"; and the Metropolitan Museum has produced a beautiful book of cats in art.

Of course the two species are very different — but so are individuals within each group. Contrary to the beliefs of those who don't know better, cats and dogs can live happily together in the same house. There is nothing so unusual in the way my dog and cat clean each other's ears regularly, and how, when one of them coughs or sneezes the other will run over as if to say (a forbidden phrase, of course), "Dear me, is something wrong? Can I get you some water?"

The problem of animal consciousness appears in cat contemplation too. (*See* Monsieur Grat, Descartes's dog.) The great French essayist Montaigne, who died four years before Descartes was born and who, if I may say so, saw this issue far more clearly than Descartes did, once wrote: "When I play with my cat, who knows whether she is not amusing herself with me more than I with her."

Twain on cat consciousness:

Cats are loose in their morals, but not consciously so. Man, in his descent from the cat, has brought the cat's looseness with him but has left the unconsciousness behind — the saving grace which excuses the cat. The cat is innocent, man is not.

Millions saw the long-running musical *Cats* based on T. S. Eliot's *Old Possum's Book of Practical Cats,* in which various cat characters spell out their personalities. The theatrical cat, for instance, anthropomorphizing like mad, tells stage anecdotes and recalls his great roles: "I used to know 70 speeches by heart." This cat understudied Dick Whittington's cat; he appeared in Shakespeare, and he even indulges in nostalgia, rhymed, about how inadequate the young are: "Now, these kittens, they do not get trained / As we did in the days when Victoria reigned."

But as Eliot so definitively put it, "A Cat is not a Dog!"

Little girls and huge dogs make beautiful friends.

Owners' Traits

Unfortunately, having a dog in your life will not automatically make you rich and famous, or even posthumously revered. And on the other hand, not all the rich and famous have or have had dogs. The overwhelming majority of dogs down through the ages have belonged to perfectly ordinary people who never made it into any encyclopaedia — they were and are just simple, unsung shepherds and suburbanites, children and professors. But as you know, in the adoring eyes of their dog, every unsung owner is/was famous beyond compare. And often enough, neglected children and neglected grown-ups have found solace in their dogs, dispensers of devoted post-graduate psychological care.

In this collection, however, it will be seen how often the dog

was truly the best friend of dominant, all-powerful personalities, of rulers whose word was law, and in our day, of stars surrounded by shrieking admirers. This hardly supports the theory that dog lovers want a creature who obeys, since the all-powerful do not need yet another creature to command. No; apparently it is lonely at the top, and even absolute rulers knew that the love and loyalty of a dog is purely for themselves and not for their position, their velvets and silver bone-and-mutton dishes. (An undocumented exception: *see* Math.) Success can easily bring suspicion and cynicism to the rich and famous. But not regarding their dogs. As so well put by a British columnist (who loves dogs), they can "reduce the greatest minds to slobbering sentimentality."

That word cynicism, by the way, comes from the Greek word for dog, and the dog became (in a negative way, it must be noted) the symbol for the sect of Greek philosophers called Cynics. The most famous of them was Diogenes, who lived in the fourth century B.C. He was extreme about his beliefs and, as you may recall, lived in a tub precisely in order to prove the unimportance of wealth and comfort. It is not known whether he lived with a dog, which is a pity. When Diogenes died (according to tradition, on the same day as Alexander the Great; *see* Peritas) a marble pillar was erected in his memory, and on it a statue of a dog.

Breeds and Breeding

Most of the dogs of most of the famous owners were indeed pure-breds, pedigreed. This has to do with cultural and kennel history; it has in some ways changed for the worse as now many people breed dogs in large numbers under poor conditions, with too much in-breeding and too much emphasis on money.

Today, the better-informed people know that a pedigreed dog will not mark you as an aristocrat, and is hardly likely to mark *you* as pure. On the contrary, the mixed breeds, the "mutts," can be more sturdy, long-lived, intelligent, and generally marvellous than some of the most expensive "pures." I grew up with pedigreed dachshunds, but dogs kept as pets today haven't the slightest opportunity, or I imagine the inclination, to demonstrate the traits for which they were presumably bred. My dachshunds never came near a badger, and although the books said they were "courageous to the point of rashness" they tended to behave like cautious, effete liberals.

Today I would never have a pedigreed dog — there are too many strays needing homes, and having so much affection and entertainment (and exercise) to give. My present mutt looks somewhat like a prehistoric pony, with small doses of Skye terrier and dachshund in there somewhere. When asked what breed she is, I say "long-haired Peruvian terrier." In any event, Spencer Tracy and Katherine Hepburn (*see* Lobo) could have a fine time at our gathering discussing the advantages of a wide genetic pool with Jane Carlyle (*see* Nero).

The reader will meet several neurotic dogs (and owners), but no viciously aggressive ones. Dangerous dogs do appear all too often in the daily media, bestowing on their owners fleeting — and absolutely forgettable — fame. Often, but not always, these dogs have been trained to be vicious, through cruelty; one particular breed, which will not be mentioned here, is said to incorporate such tendencies.

Barbara Woodhouse, England's *grande dame* of dog training (over 20,000, with of course their owners), believes that in general "there are no bad dogs, only bad owners." But she has of course seen situations in which hitherto "good" dogs will suddenly maul their owners; and cases turn up of puppies, born into loving homes and provided with the best of everything, who simply turn nasty. Such dogs must be destroyed.

In other words, some dogs — exactly like some people — are simply born crazy. If there can be occasional defects in the human brain, and never mind all the affection and proper education, then why not also in the canine brain?

This collection started very simply, and I never dreamed it would lead to a millennium-spanning party. It began when I happened to learn that Schopenhauer, the German philosopher once greatly revered and now largely forgotten, had only one friend in his life: his poodle. The dog's name was Atman (which takes us to Hindu mysticism), and he was the pessimistic thinker's "trustiest mate," as the *Britannica* puts it. You will meet him among the A's, right after Errol Flynn's schnauzer Arno. Schopenhauer hated women; Flynn loved them a bit too much. But, we are told on good authority, he loved his schnauzer more.

Somehow, the idea of Schopenhauer's poodle struck me as a beguiling bridge to philosophy, and via that bridge to much else. How right I was. Soon after meeting Atman, I stumbled upon Geist, one of the dachshunds that belonged to Matthew Arnold, the great Victorian writer. I once loved Arnold devotedly, but had, I am afraid, forgotten him in the welter of information of our bright new world. His dachshunds brought us together again, and they in turn unearthed quite an Action Group of other dachshunds who romp in these pages.

So I began to re-read Arnold. The Victorians are making a comeback among critics in our post-modern literary world because it suddenly seems interesting that the Victorians had two opposing views of what was happening as their century drew to a close: everything better and better, or then again, probably not.

From Matthew Arnold, then, we take the following four lines from one of his poems. In stately cadence, they serve as a formal invitation to everyone coming to our party, and they explain why we can have a celebration for dogs and their distinguished owners who lived so far apart in what is called Time–Space:

> *And we, whose ways were unlike here,*
> *May then more neighbouring courses ply:*
> *May to each other be brought near,*
> *And greet across infinity.*

List of Famous Owners

Alcibiades (*see* "Hermes")
Alexander the Great (*see* Peritas)
Arnold, Matthew (*see* Geist)
Bankhead, Tallulah (*see* Delores)
Bismarck, Otto von (*see* Tyras)
Browning, Elizabeth Barrett (*see* Flush)
Bush, Barbara (*see* Millie)
Byron, Lord (*see* Boatswain)
Carlyle, Jane and Thomas (*see* Nero)
Charles II (*see* "Nell" and "Gwynne")
Chesterton, G. K. (*see* Quoodle)
Christie, Agatha (*see* Tony)
Churchill, Winston (*see* Rufus)
Colette (*see* Belle Aude)
Coolidge, President Calvin (*see* Rob Roy)
Descartes, René (*see* Monsieur Grat)
Du Chatelet, Emilie, Voltaire's mistress (*see* Dear Love)
Edward VII (*see* Caesar)
Ehrlich, Paul (*see* "Salvarsan")
Elizabeth, Empress of Austria (*see* Shadow)
Elizabeth II (*see* Harris)
Flynn, Errol (*see* Arno)
Frederick the Great (*see* Alcmene)
Freud, Sigmund (*see* Jofi)
Haile Selassie (*see* Lulu)
Hardy, Thomas (*see* Wessie)
Hearst, William Randolph (*see* Helena)
Hepburn, Katherine, with Spencer Tracy (*see* Lobo)
Hitchcock, Alfred (*see* Sarah)
Hogarth, William (*see* Trump)
Institutions:
   His Master's Voice records (*see* Nipper)
   The Pall Mall Gazette (*see* Lobengula)

Johnson, President Lyndon (*see* Him and Her)
Kipling, Rudyard (*see* Vixen)
Landor, Walter Savage (*see* Pomero and Giallo)
Liberace (*see* Baby Boy)
Liebermann, Max (*see* Pladumini)
Luciano, Lucky (*see* "Mafia")
Maeterlinck, Maurice de (*see* Pelleas)
Mann, Thomas (*see* Bashan)
Mary Stuart, Queen of Scots (*see* "Bonny")
Mithras (*see* "Zodi")
Monroe, Marilyn (*see* Maf)
Munthe, Axel (*see* Gorm)
Nixon, President Richard (*see* Checkers)
Odysseus (*see* Argos)
Parker, Dorothy (*see* Eiko von Blutenberg and Robinson)
Picasso, Pablo (*see* Lump)
Reagan, President Ronald (*see* Lucky)
Richard II (*see* Math)
Roosevelt, President Franklin D. (*see* Fala)
Rousseau, Jean Jacques (*see* "Eloise")
Rupert, Prince (*see* Boy)
Schweitzer, Albert (*see* "Ohren")
Schopenhauer, Arthur (*see* Atman)
Simonides (*see* Lycas)
Stein, Gertrude (*see* Basket)
Steinbeck, John (*see* Charley)
Susann, Jacqueline (*see* Josephine)
Tobit (apocryphal book) (*see* "Tobi")
Tutankhamen (*see* Abuwitiyuw)
Ullman, Liv (*see* Pet)
Verdi, Giuseppi (*see* Pretin)
Wordsworth, William (*see* Music)
Xanthippus, father of Pericles (*see* "Xanti")

(Dogs' names in quotation marks indicate that true name is unknown; they have been bestowed here as mnemonic devices.)

ABUWITIYUW — Hunting hound of King Tutankhamen, ruler of Egypt around 1350 B.C., whose tomb was discovered at Luxor in 1922 (*see* Gorm). When Abuwitiyuw died, he was royally mummified — "wrapped in fine linen and laid to rest in a coffin, perfumed and anointed with preservative ointments." A model of the dog was found near the entrance of his young master's tomb.

King Tutankhamen was the son-in-law and successor of the heretic King Amenhotep IV (Akhnaton), who worshipped the sun. Tutankhamen married his daughter and came to the throne when he was about 12 years old. A "helpless puppet" in the hands of the priestly party, he died about six years later. His fame is due entirely to the discovery of his richly-furnished but relatively unimportant tomb.

But at least he had his "Abu" to enjoy: the hapless boy-king is said to have "loved to watch this graceful hound leaping with joy at the sight of a gazelle and enjoyed having him as his companion on the hunt."

Dogs (and cats) were very much part of the life of Egypt more than 4,000 years ago, having their place in religion, in hunting, and companionship. Two distinct types of early Egyptian dogs are apparent from sculpture and monuments — slender dogs of the greyhound types, and short-legged doggies resembling terriers and (of all things) dachshunds.

Abu was by no means a rarity among mummified dogs in ancient Egypt. According to Herodotus, when a dog died in Egypt the whole household often went into deep mourning; "heads were shaved, food went untouched." After embalming and burial in a special section, the bereaved owners and attendants "scourged themselves and wailed loudly."

Psychologist Stanley Coren, who has closely investigated the intelligence of various breeds, has even tested what he calls the "Pharaoh hound" (which must be a fairly rare breed, since a short, unscientific survey has failed to reveal anyone who has ever encountered one).

The Pharaoh hound nevertheless appears on Professor Coren's table, listing no less than 135 breeds in order of declining rank "for obedience and working intelligence." King Tut's dog is not too far down, sharing the #35th spot with five other breeds — affenpinschers, silky terriers, miniature pinschers, English setters, and clumber spaniels.

We may be glad that Abuwitiyuw made life a little happier for his posthumously-famous royal owner. And nobody would expect a poor little rich dog to perform (on an IQ chart) with the brilliance of a border collie from hard-working Scotland, who leads the list — or with a poodle (*see* Atman) who comes in second. On the other hand, he does not rank nearly as low as the basenji, which was also known in ancient Egypt and is a small "barkless" dog with a silky coat. The presumably uneducable basenji closes the list with the also hapless Afghan hound (from Afghanistan, far far away from Scotland and Germany).

ALCMENE, also THISBE, DIANA, PHILLIS, GIGAS, PAX, SUPERBE, HASENFUSS, AMOURETTE, ARSINOE, and BICHE — The 15 dearly beloved greyhounds of Frederick II (1712–86), King of Prussia. (These do not add up to 15, as you may have noticed; this is because "Old Fritz," as Frederick the Great was also known, named three of the greyhounds Alcmene, and gave two others the names Thisbe and Diana.) Most of the names he chose are, of course, from Greek mythology, and the stories they recall (see below), with their unusual sexual alliances, were certainly not lost on this remarkable absolute ruler.

Frederick was far ahead of his time in many ways, including social outlook. Loved, feared, honoured, and cursed, he combined a love of culture and philosophy with a long career of diplomatic and military successes — and losses. His own youth, however, was as difficult as that of any abused slum child, so that in such new fields as psychobiography, this Frederick has few rivals.

His friendship and correspondence with Voltaire (*see* Dear Love) is part of history. But his intense relationship with his greyhounds lasted longer, and was, naturally, free of ultimate jealousies. Several of the greyhounds shared Frederick's bed during his last lonely years.

By royal command, all the greyhounds lie buried near each other in two semicircular rows close to Frederick's own grave, which is at his magnificent pleasure palace at Sans Souci, near Potsdam in former East Germany. Today, 200 years and many wars later, the inscriptions on the dogs' graves can barely be deciphered.

The servants who took care of the royal dogs were required to address them as *Sie*, the German polite form of address, as distinguished from the familiar *du*. The greyhounds had the run of the palace at Sans Souci and occupied a place of honour in every way. Like most dogs, they liked sitting on the best sofas — marvellous velvets and tapestries, which they usually dirtied. Unlike most dogs, these were permitted their whims.

We even know something of the menus they enjoyed: cold

roasts, cakes, butter-rolls, fresh rich milk. Modern vets would frown on such a diet, but no dog in his right mind would refuse. The special favourites, such as Biche and Alcmene, had their own chairs next to Frederick at mealtimes. It was then his custom to take pieces of roast meat with the royal fingers, place them on the tablecloth to cool, and then present them to the dog at his side.

Frederick's own early years were traumatically different. The son of Frederick William I, he was despised by his father because the unhappy boy loved literature and music, secretly learned Latin, preferred French culture to anything German, and refused to hunt and shoot. His father, seeing his son "absorbed in frivolous and effeminate amusements," treated him abominably. The son finally decided to run away with two friends who were lieutenants in his father's army. They were captured, Frederick was imprisoned, and one of the lieutenants was beheaded in his presence.

"If he kicks or rears again," said the super-Prussian father, "he shall forfeit the crown, and even . . . life itself."

Frederick had good reason to dislike much of the human race (except for intellectuals and artists). As he wrote to his sister, who shared many of his views:

It must be a consolation to the animals to see that humans, who are endowed with intelligence, are often no better than they are.

Attributed to Frederick, and very similar to the view expressed by Byron (see Boatswain), is his saying regarding dogs; that "they have all the good qualities of humans without any of their faults."

The royal Prussian father treated both his children violently. Daughter Wilhelmine wrote: "The King's anger against my brother and myself reached such a pitch that, with the exception of the hours for meals, we were banished from his presence." Once, during such a meal, the King threw a plate at his son's head, and then another at his daughter, who recalled that she "also happily escaped, but then torrents of abuse followed. As my brother and I passed near him, he hit out at us with his crutch."

On his father's orders, Frederick married a cousin of Maria

Theresa when he was 20. "I will marry to obey him; after that I will shove my wife into a corner and live after my own fancy." According to Thomas Carlyle (*see* Nero), who wrote an admiring, six-volume biography of Frederick, the marriage was never consummated, and Frederick in turn treated his wife "brutally." There were no children.

His tastes were clearly otherwise. After his father died in 1740 and he ascended the throne, Frederick continued his correspondence with Voltaire, whom he considered his teacher, and whose lack of religious faith he shared. Early in his reign, Frederick issued an order that

All religions must be tolerated, and the government must see to it that none of them makes unjust encroachments on any other, for in this country every man must get to heaven in his own way.

To Voltaire, six days after he took his father's place on the throne, Frederick wrote:

My lot is changed. I have witnessed the last moments of a king, his agony, his death. On coming to the throne I had no need of that lesson to be disgusted with the vanity of human grandeur . . . I beg you will see in me nothing but a zealous citizen, a rather skeptical philosopher, and a really faithful friend . . .

Frederick set up an "openly homosexual" court at his beautiful new palace, Sans Souci ("Without Cares"), attracting "middle-class intellectuals and open sodomites." Frederick played the flute like a professional, wrote poetry and, later, military history; his works fill 30 volumes.

In addition to strengthening and closely administering Prussia (and answering every letter on the day it was received), he planned parties for his exclusively male society. Supper was in a room decorated principally by a painting, designed by Frederick, "of an orgy in which a crowd of humans and animals were all making love." He gave up Christianity, and "no woman or priest ever set foot" in carefree Sans Souci. (Most of the greyhounds, it may be noted, were females.)

For his time a very liberal and enlightened king, Frederick began his reign with programmes to help the oppressed population. In due course, through many wars, alliances, invasions, and counter-alliances, he made Prussia into a great power. As Carlyle put it admiringly, he displayed "great military genius and perseverance in the face of great odds." He was very interested in the American Revolution and particularly admired George Washington.

The year before ascending the throne, Frederick published, anonymously, a refutation of Machiavelli; Voltaire wrote the preface and corrected the proofs. The secret of its authorship soon

emerged, and "readers joined Voltaire in hailing the advent of a philosopher-king."

Later, Frederick invited Voltaire to live at his court; their relationship was, in a sense, a battle between Voltaire's mistress and Frederick for Voltaire's soul. (She won.) Voltaire considered bringing his mistress to Sans Souci, but decided that in that company she would be like "a fish out of water."

With the years, Frederick grew colder and more aloof, remaining "the terror of Europe and the darling of philosophers." His cynicism made him a master of diplomacy, of military campaigns, and of conversation. A prince visiting Sans Souci described his talk as "encyclopaedic — the fine arts, war, medicine, literature, religion, philosophy, morals, history, legislation . . ."

This is not the place to replay the many bloody wars and shifting alliances that made Prussia, under Frederick's absolute rule, a world power. Instead, we will here point to the romantic side of his character, as reflected in his choice of names for the greyhounds. Frustrated in lasting human love, and certainly not a man for marriage, he three times picked the name Alcmene for three of his favourites.

And who was Alcmene? The Greek name means "might of the moon," or "mighty in wrath." In Greek mythology Alcmene appears often in the accounts of Hercules' labours — he was, after all, her son. She was the wife of Amphitryon, King of Argos, which in no way prevented her from becoming the paramour of Zeus. She was the last mortal woman Zeus embraced, and he was the father of her son Hercules. After the death of her husband, a mere mortal, Alcmene married a kind of relative, Rhadamanthus, who was a son of Zeus and Europa; when he died, Zeus appointed him a judge in Hades. Not a bad three-time name for the dogs of a complex, unhappy, absolute ruler who expressed in so many ways his absolute contempt for mankind.

Voltaire at Sans Souci reads to Frederick and bored Alcmene.

"ALPHONSE" — Lapdog that rarely left the lap of Alphonse de Lamartine (1790 – 1869), romantic French poet, traveller, statesman, historical and biographical writer (61 volumes).

"Alphonse," our name for this lapdog (breed unspecified; it might have been a toy spaniel or terrier), is chosen to help us remember the name of a once hugely famous personality. By the age of 30, Lamartine was widely known throughout Europe for his lyrical — and sentimental — verse, which was considered a graceful but also passionate continuation of Byron's. (Interestingly, the very small and somewhat deformed Byron chose a huge Newfoundland, Boatswain [q.v.], as his favourite dog, while Lamartine, proud of his looks, picked a tiny breed.)

As a measure of Lamartine's forgotten fame, it may be recalled that when he ran for the National Assembly in 1848 — that volatile period of revolution and the Second Republic in France — his opponent Balzac (still fairly well remembered) received a total of 20 votes. Lamartine received 159,800 in Paris alone. And another measure: the owner of a large bookstore in Paris, when asked for Lamartine's biography, replied that he had none, and that it was the first such request in 30 years.

Little "Alphonse," the small dog, travelled with his devoted master to the Middle East in 1832. Lamartine had left the foreign service, where he had been secretary of the embassy at Naples, and had married a rich Englishwoman. In Syria, Lamartine (without his wife, but with "Alphonse") went to visit Lady Hester Stanhope, "Queen of Lebanon" as Lamartine called her. This distinguished Englishwoman, niece of William Pitt, was living a dazzlingly eccentric life among the Druse, on a Syrian mountaintop. Among her retinue were two white horses, with whom she was awaiting the Messiah, and many cats, whom she considered holy animals.

Lamartine wrote effusively about Lady Hester in his *Souvenirs of the Orient.* He did not realize that she later made fun of his cuddly involvement with "Alphonse," always there on his lap, and the constant object of a shower of sweet nothings. But he "blushed with pleasure" when the astute Lady Hester flattered

Alphonse de Lamartine.

Lamartine by admiring his fine posture, his delicate fingers (as they tickled the ears of "Alphonse") and his beautiful feet: both he and she, the Lady said, had "Arab feet."

Born to a noble Catholic family, the only son of six children, Lamartine grew up in the country and the romance of nature was always with him. His early literary works covered the usual menu of loneliness, resignation, and tragic love.

As a self-described "democratic conservative" who wanted to place "the muse in the service of politics," Lamartine was briefly much in the public eye; but he lacked realism and practical sense, and the era was far too unpredictable for a sentimental amateur. Politically, his course was the opposite of the usual: with time, he became more liberal.

In his later years he produced a huge flow of writing because he needed the money. Considered of little value, these volumes cover everything from Russian history to Cromwell, Shakespeare, Caesar, and Rousseau (*see* "Eloise"). At his peak, his works were translated into many languages, and a few years after his death a statue was erected to him in Passy, with much fanfare.

Readers a century later are likely to come across Lamartine only through Lady Hester Stanhope, whose biography (also translated) appeared in 1953. That book makes the further doggy point that another visitor to Lady Hester in 1837, the eccentric and also once very famous Prince Pückler, was careful *not* to bring his beloved dog Chameleon with him for the obligatory visit, and for *his* published account of the Lady.

In one of his best works, *The Lake*, Lamartine writes about a visit to a village where he was once happy with his mistress:

O time, suspend your flight, and you, happy hours, stay your feet! Let us savour the swift delights of our life's loveliest days!

What marvellous phrases little "Alphonse" heard whispered in his furry ears a century and a half ago, in that once famous lap! And even better, for a top lapdog, in the original French: *O temps, suspends ton vol; et vous, heures propices! Suspendez votre cours . . .*

ARGOS — Hound of Odysseus, hero of Homer's epic. When Odysseus (his Greek name, meaning "angry"; Latin Ulysses) finally returned home to Ithaca after 20 years' wandering following the Trojan War, he disguised himself as a beggar in order to spy on the many suitors of his wife Penelope. Odysseus' loyal hound Argos (also spelled Argus) was the only one who recognized him.

As Homer describes this vignette in the gory homecoming scene, Odysseus reaches his palace court and finds old Argos, once a famous hunting hound,

> stretched on a dunghill, mangy, decrepit, and tormented by fleas. Argos wagged his raw stump of a tail and drooped his tattered ears in recognition of Odysseus, who covertly brushed away a tear as Argos expired.

All educated readers once knew the devious adventures of Odysseus and his comrades during the war against Troy, which was waged in order to recover the beautiful Helen, who had been carried away by the son of Priam, the King of Troy. Homer told it all in the great epic poem filling 24 books, the *Iliad*, which has long been called "the first Greek novel." The details of the 20 long years of Odysseus' return voyage fill the *Odyssey*.

We are told on good authority that "there is no reason to suppose Odysseus other than a real man, renowned for his skill and resource, about whom in the course of centuries numerous fictions have gathered."

As for his wife Penelope, she has become a symbol of patience and cleverness in putting off her suitors during the long absence, "one hundred and twelve insolent young princes" who were couring the Queen and "disporting themselves in Odysseus' palace, drinking his wine . . . and seducing his maidservants."

Penelope, who cannot have been in the first flush of youth, put them off with the famous story of needing first to finish weaving a shroud for her late father-in-law. She wove by day and unravelled it all every night, from which we have the saying "Penelope's Web," for a never-finished task.

Actually, a close reading of some of Robert Graves' and other

Irreverent view of Odysseus and Argos by Honoré Daumier.

notes to Homer tells us that Penelope was not Odysseus' first choice: he really wanted to marry the beautiful Helen, the cause of all the trouble, but had no chance.

Nor did he want to go off to fight the Trojans. In a famous

scene as the expedition was being organized, Odysseus pretended to be mad — "ploughing with an ass and an ox yoked together and flinging salt over his shoulder . . ." The recruiting party, suspecting a ruse, put his infant son on the ground before the team. Odysseus quickly pulled in the animals to avoid killing his son, and therefore had to go off to war.

Was Argos there, a happy puppy, watching it all? And another unanswerable question: what are we to think of faithful-wife Penelope for neglecting her husband's loyal old hound and leaving him, sick and uncared for, on that dungheap?

In the translation of the *Odyssey* by Pope, on which he worked for 12 years and which was severely criticized at the time by those who knew their Greek better than most of us do today, the Argos story is related in these lines:

> *He knew his lord — he knew, and strove to meet.*
> *In vain he strove to crawl, and kiss his feet.*
> *Yet (all he could) his tail, his ears, his eyes,*
> *Salute his master and confess his joys.*
> *Soft pity touch'd the mighty master's soul,*
> *Adown his cheek a tear unbidden stole.*
> *The dog whom Fate had granted to behold*
> *His lord, when twenty tedious years had roll'd,*
> *Takes a last look and having seen him, dies;*
> *So closed forever faithful Argus' eyes.*

ARNO — Schnauzer and constant companion of Errol Flynn (1909 – 59), rip-roaring, colourful, charming, athletic, hard-drinking, self-destructive movie star and enthusiastic womanizer. According to his biographer, Michael Freedland, Flynn gave to Arno the "absolute devotion he could never show to a woman," or to his many male friends either. As one of the closest, David Niven put it, "The great thing about Errol was, you always knew precisely where you stood with him because he always lets you down."

Flynn let himself down too — on drink, on drugs, from pot, and ascending to heroin and opium, long before the rank-and-file took them up. He never even considered being "supportive" of his endless stream of women, and remained enthusiastically polygamous to the end.

With Arno it was a different story. This well-connected schnauzer, a gift to Flynn from a Hollywood producer, became a "Hollywood fixture" and went everywhere that Flynn went — to the studio, to nightclubs, to his master's beloved yacht *Sirocco*.

Fearless Flynn even fought a duel because of Arno. It happened, in true Western fashion, at a local bar in rural California where Niven and Flynn were making a film. It was *The Charge of the Light Brigade*, with Olivia de Havilland, whom Flynn loved — for a while.

As Niven tells the tale, the owner of the bar, "a large ox-like moron of permanent belligerence," objected to all dogs, "especially those who lifted their legs on the corner of his building." To teach them not to do so, he installed a metal on the door-post connected to an electric battery:

Poor Arno came bouncing along, as we were about to enter the bar, and lifted his leg in the danger area. The amber arc completed the circuit and the luckless animal, collecting a high-voltage shock in his offending organ, was hurled into the air and went careering down the street howling with pain and terror.

Flynn strode into the bar, and the place fell quiet. The customers were evenly matched, local cow-hands and ranchers and tough stunt doubles from our picture. All prudently remained on their stools while Flynn took the barman apart. It was a bloody battle, Flynn revelled in it, and Arno was the last dog in Lone Pine to get shock treatment in his private parts.

Flynn was born in Tasmania, Australia. An early photograph shows him aged about four, a beautiful little boy in a home-made tent, with a small dog at his side. Adventurous and lazy from an early age, Flynn was nothing like his father, a professor of biology. The son preferred sports, and was Australian Junior Tennis Champion. At 17, he was off to New Guinea to look for gold. After a wild series of exotic episodes he went to England and, by chance, found himself in a repertory company and then (by lying about his experience) in films. And then on to Hollywood.

During his lifetime with Arno, Flynn was married to Lili Damita, a ravishingly beautiful French film star; he called her Tiger Lil, and their marriage has been described as "a marathon wrestling match." They were divorced in 1942.

That same year, Flynn went on trial for statutory rape of two

teen-age girls; a good lawyer got him acquitted. But as Flynn enjoyed saying, he liked "his whiskey old, and his girls young." And as his colleague-in-fun-and-films Niven put it, "Looking back on many weekends aboard *Sirocco*, I could not remember any 'crew members' flashing their birth certificates as they trooped expectantly up the gang-plank." And who was one of the young students, back in those pre-feminist, Family Value days, who held proud membership in the A.B.C.D.E.F. (American Boys' Club for the Defence of Errol Flynn)? Why, none other than William F. Buckley, Jr.

The schnauzer as love object has attributes which might give it the edge over eager teen-agers and flamboyant French stars. The traits usually listed include "intelligence and dependability" — and yes, liveliness as well. No mention of suicidal impulses (see below). The name comes from the Swiss-German, and the breed is closely connected to the pinscher. Like the Airedale's, the rough coat must be plucked.

Flynn loved his yacht much more than he loved his home. Yet it was on the yacht that Flynn lost Arno. On one outing, the dog jumped overboard from the deck and vanished. Acquired neurotic self-destruction? (*See* Flush.) As Freedland describes the episode, when the dog's washed-up body was identified, Flynn "could not bear to look at the dead remains of a friend that had meant so much to him in life. He buried its collar in his garden at Mulholland Drive."

In the Hollywood gossip columns, it was seen differently:

> Errol Flynn, whose love for his dog Arno has been much heralded, didn't even bother to try to rescue the dog, or to get his body when it was washed up on shore. That's how much he meant to him.

This attack, a "particularly nauseating" one, according to Niven, and patently a lie, was written by columnist Jimmy Fidler. With Niven, Flynn spent a day looking for Fidler, and finally saw him at night at, naturally, an In nightclub, the Mocambo. Flynn was outraged not only by the Arno story, but also by the attitude of Fidler, an arch-isolationist, towards Hollywood's British

Colony before America's entrance into the war. Flynn played war heroes in movies, but was turned down for Army service because of a bad heart. He was also accused of anti-Semitism, and even became the subject of an investigation, whose findings were "inconclusive."

The affair at the Mocambo was anything but inconclusive. When Flynn saw the columnist he hit him on the face with his open hand, saying, "I won't dignify you with a fist." Fidler, who had just testified before a Senate committee on the need to "avoid intervention," went down with a thud. Flynn shouted at him that he had told one lie too many. And Mrs Fidler "stuck a fork in Flynn's ear."

The columnist sued Flynn for assault; the judge merely made the actor promise that he would not punch the man again.

Flynn's last years, when he was separated from his third wife, were filled with more brawls, carousing, drinking, stimulants, travels with a new yacht. His health deteriorated: it would have done so years earlier with a less vital man.

A few hours before his death, under doctor's orders to lie down and rest, Flynn insisted that all he wanted to do was to "sit with interesting people and talk. So for two hours he romanced about the glories of Hollywood, holding his small audience spellbound as he mimicked Jack Warner and John Barrymore." He died that night.

His only son Sean, by Tiger Lil, no less handsome than his father, became a press photographer. He was listed "missing, presumed dead" in Vietnam.

ATMAN, also ATMA — Poodle and only friend of German philosopher Arthur Schopenhauer (1788–1860). Pessimistic, morbid, paranoid (Schopenhauer, not, as far as is known, the poodle), he has been described as one of the most intelligent men of his time.

Atman, a term in Hindu literature, refers to the "unchanged and persistent identity which continues in the midst of all change"; also "world soul," and is thus an appropriate name for Schopenhauer's poodle. The term comes from the Upanishads, in Hindu literature, which was among the many fields studied by Schopenhauer. The Upanishads were part of the Veda (we're back around the year 1000 B.C.) and their purpose was "to bring peace and freedom to the anxious human spirit."

So, again: Atman is a good name for a poodle who was a melancholy philosopher's best friend. But the wits of Frankfurt, where Schopenhauer spent his last 30 years in two rented rooms with Atman, called the dog Schopenhauer Junior.

"If there were no dogs," Schopenhauer once said, "I would not wish to live." Atman died in 1849, and Schopenhauer, who lived on for another 11 years, mourned him deeply.

But he also said funny, if cynical things. Like: "If we were not all so interested in ourselves, life would be so uninteresting that none of us would be able to endure it."

Little Arthur grew up with a love for dogs — there were two small dogs in his prosperous parental home. He had much more trouble with his family. His mother, unhappy in her marriage to her prosaic business-man husband, became a very popular writer of romantic novels, and considered her son her rival. Arthur's sister Adele, also a writer and mover in literary circles, wrote analyses of Goethe. Schopenhauer's father is believed to have committed suicide by throwing himself into the Hamburg Canal; his paternal grandmother was mentally disturbed.

After her husband's death the widow Schopenhauer moved to Weimar, came out in favour of free love, and assembled a small literary salon. Goethe was fond of her, though she did not enjoy hearing from him that her son would be a famous man; she was

sure that "there could not be two geniuses in the same family."
She once wrote to Arthur:

You are a terrible burden and quite unbearable, and I consider it
nearly impossible to live with you. All your good qualities are dimmed
by your super-intelligence, because you can't overcome the vicious urge
to know everything better. And with this you embitter all those around
you . . .

At the height of one of their quarrels, the mother threw her
philosopher-son down the stairs, after which Arthur assured his
mother that her name would, in the future, be known only
through him. He soon left Weimar and never saw his mother
again, although she lived for another 24 years.

Schopenhauer's attitude towards women was certainly formed
by his relationship to his mother: he despised them, while being
obsessed by sex. Much of what he wrote on this subject, according
to his biographers, was "unfit for publication." Love, he believed,
is a means of deception (except with regard to dogs); it cannot
last, "and therefore philosophers do not marry." Needless to say,
Schopenhauer never did, and lived all his life without friends or
family — except for Atman, and books.

One fundamental fault of the female character, Schopenhauer
wrote, "is that it has no sense of justice . . . Women may have
meaningful talent, but not genius because they will always remain
subjective." There is something in this, to be sure; but since when
have men been totally objective? Particularly pessimists with
unhappy childhoods?

Schopenhauer's main work, *Die Welt als Wille und Vorstellung*
("The World as Will and Representation") was published in 1819,
to little acclaim. It would make a very poor TV series, although
Will would have been a good name for a dog. Its pessimistic
philosophy, put very briefly (and not too coherently): Will, which
is self-conscious in man, is the only reality. It finds its equivalent
in the unconscious forces of nature. It is what creates the world —
and the world is a malignant illusion that seduces us into
reproducing and perpetuating life. Chastity is the duty of man,

with the purpose of terminating this evil. God, free-will, and immortality are illusions. And so on, all set forth in two volumes with great clarity and organization.

Towards the end of his life, Schopenhauer finally began to receive the acclaim he had so long wished for, and attracted increasing notice. Wagner sent him a copy of the *Ring* in acknowledgement of his philosophy. He became nearly happy, and enjoyed playing the flute after supper. In 1858, on his 70th birthday, greetings came from all corners of the earth. It was not too soon. Two years later, apparently in the best of health, he died while eating breakfast.

A century after the appearance of *Dies Welt als Wille und*

(above) German poodle with French haircut.

Vorstellung — but still before the advent of TV — Thomas Mann (*see* Bashan) wrote an important essay on Schopenhauer, to whom he felt deeply indebted. Mann's generation, it has been suggested, was growing doubtful over the "validity of the individual, the suspicion that the apparent multiplicity of the human race is only a deceit." To Schopenhauer, as Mann saw him, most men are "naïve egoists" while the

enlightened man . . . perceives that the line of demarcation between himself and anyone else is illusory; each man, each being in the created universe, is a stage in the disintegration of the One, Schopenhauer's Will . . . which is a raging flux desperately articulating itself into the reaches of time and space.

(above) Schopenhauer as a young man, portrait by Ludwig Sigismund Ruhl.

Atman, meet Bashan — you are both really One.

Some sayings of Schopenhauer:

I am convinced that a man's ability to endure noise is in inverse ratio to his intelligence. (Noted long before the amplifier and other modern aids.)

To be alone is the fate of all great minds — a fate deplored at times, but still always chosen as the less grievous of two evils.

The less one has to do with women, the better . . . They are not even a "necessary evil" . . . In their hearts, women believe that the purpose of men is to earn money and bring it home to them . . . The luxury and waste of the women in the court of Louis XIII was apparently the basic cause of the corruption that brought on the French Revolution.

Finally, a word about the Atman as poodle. This breed gets high marks for intelligence in all tests; it is said to be closely related to sheep dogs but classified in the non-sporting group.

They are often called French poodles, probably because of their absurd hair-cuts. But this is incorrect. The poodle is originally an athletic, sturdy, water-loving German dog, and the name "poodle" is related to "puddle" — from the Low-German term *pudeln*, meaning to splash in water.

Yet even in Germany more than a century ago, poodles were already sporting those expensive hair-cuts (and, for better or for worse, the toy breed was already available). Atman, as seen with his master in contemporary depictions, was always clipped in the latest fashion. Is it curious that Schopenhauer, given his views of being In socially, would have wanted his closest friend done up with a pom-pom tail and ruffles on all four ankles?

In any event, poodles make up a goodly contingent in this collection. Atman might have much to communicate to Basket (q.v.), whose mistress, although a female of her species, would in no way have terrified Schopenhauer.

Schopenhauer and Atman, caricature by Wilhelm Busch.

BABY BOY — Poodle beloved by Liberace (1919 – 86), brilliant showman, flamboyantly dressed, glittery-fingered, multi-million-aire piano-playing idol of older women for several decades.

Baby Boy has been picked here nearly at random, although his name heads the list alphabetically among the 17 dogs who shared the popular pianist's life. There were six other poodles (two of them toys), a cocker spaniel, a schnauzer, a chow, a Lhasa Apso, two Shar-peis, and two undesignated breeds.

Liberace lived to the (jewelled) hilt, and could well afford to. His income, based solely on his ten fingers and his wildly creative, and humorous, imagination, averaged $5 million per year for over 25 years. A huge crowd-drawer all his life, he sold out 18 concerts in 21 days at Radio City Music Hall in New York the year before his death, grossing $2.5 million in those three weeks.

Baby Boy and the other resident dogs naturally also lived opulent lives with their doting owner. This flashy poodle ate supper every night with Liberace, sitting at the dining room table in his own chair, with his own silver bowl and wearing his own jewelled collar. We may assume that Baby Boy and the other dogs knew better than to bark while the master was practising, having somehow learned the value of silence from their fellow-poodle Atman (q.v.).

Liberace was ahead of his time in correctly evaluating the modern popular public's attention span. He learned early the secret of "cutting out the dull parts" and giving the audience what he called his "*Readers' Digest* versions" of popular works, whipping fabulously through Chopin's Minute Waltz in 37 seconds, and through Tchaikovsky's First Piano Concerto, not known for its brevity, in just four minutes.

He also learned early that clothes make the man, or at least the celebrity. It started as a joke. For a 1952 concert at the Hollywood Bowl he wore white tails "so they could see me in the back row." For Las Vegas, he added a gold lamé jacket. As he put it afterwards, "Wow! They crawled out of the woodwork when they saw it. What started as a gag became a trademark."

It also became a precedent for subsequent super-popular performers: Elvis Presley (*his* dogs were called Brutus and Snoopy) was soon wearing gold lamé suits, and so were Elvis impersonators.

But who could impersonate, or even afford, Liberace's eventual wardrobe? (It included a silver-plum lamé cape with an eight-foot train of pink feathers, a $300,000 Norwegian blue-fox cape, with a 16-foot train, a sequined drum-major's uniform?) And who but Liberace could perform like a wizard during two-hour concerts, broken only by short breaks for costume changes, unbowed by those capes weighing 175 pounds and undaunted by the jeers of serious critics? His flying fingers flashing not just one huge ring, or two, but five or six?

"People ask me how I can play with all those rings," and I reply, "Very well, thank you." This is one of the many quips in Liberace's picture-autobiography published late in his life. As has been astutely said, "He seemed to have so much fun making fun of himself that it was hard for others to make fun of him."

Even more important: few, if any, of his "serious" critics had played the Liszt Piano Concerto with the Chicago Symphony at the age of 17, as young Liberace had. He grew up with the classic piano repertoire, but also played honky-tonk tunes in cocktail bars as a teen-ager, under the name "Walter Busterkeys."

Born Wladsiu Valentino Liberace in a small Wisconsin town, "Lee," as his friends called him, stopped using his first and middle names early in his career. Paderewski, whom young Lee idolized, had done the same, and "didn't achieve fame until he dropped his first name."

His father, a grocer, had played French horn in John Philip Sousa's concert band, and his mother played the piano; little Liberace began piano lessons when he was four years old.

He stumbled early on the secret of his spectacular success, "a unique blend of Beethoven and the Beer Barrel Polka," soon enhanced by that incredible wardrobe and his trademark candelabrum on the piano.

Then in mid-career he suddenly went conservative: he cut his hair and dispensed with the photogenic frills. What happened? The audiences diminished, the bookings dropped. So he returned to his sequins and capes: why be stupid and desert your incredible niche when you can so easily carry on with mansions, rhinestones, and Rolls Royces?

Always controversially in the public eye, Liberace was sued in 1982 for $113 million, for breach of financial promise by his "chauffeur, bodyguard, and companion," as such functionaries were called. The suit was settled shortly before Liberace's death for $35,000. At about the same time, front-page stories in Las Vegas, where he was then living, claimed that Liberace was dying of AIDS.

A man of many talents as well as of many dogs, Liberace grew orchids, liked to cook, made hand-painted ties for the Minneapolis Lakers basketball team, and invented, of all things, an "invisible toilet." He opened his Hollywood mansion to the public, admission fees going to the Liberace Foundation for the Creative and Performing Arts, to help young artists.

With all this, who knows whether Baby Boy might not have been happier eating bones on the floor from a plastic plate, together with some baby girl — Liberace's toy poodle Suzette, perhaps, or even his West Highland terrier, Lady Di. Might he not have preferred a Baby Girl, even of mixed breed?

BALTIQUE — Dearly beloved, dearly loving black Labrador of François Mitterand (1916−96), third president of the Fifth French Republic. In his last will and testament, Mitterand asked that Baltique should walk in his funeral procession, thus providing a contemporary shadow of the royal funeral of Edward VII (*see* Caesar).

Of Baltique, who accompanied his master nearly everywhere, Mitterand once said, "He is the only living creature who never asked me any favours."

He hardly needed to. Baltique dined off Sèvres porcelain dishes, drank only mineral water, had two attendants and a car and chauffeur at his disposal. Mitterand addressed him in the polite French form, *Vous* (*see* Alcmene).

Mitterand was passionately devoted to women, dogs, literature, and his own often problematic image of himself. When he died, the world press, in our contemporary open style, gave much coverage to the presidential mistress of many years, and to their daughter, who also attended the funeral. Baltique, too, was photographed, and the details of his mourning for his master duly gave rise to analyses of the way animals mourn. Baltique became listless, refused to eat, and expressed his grief unmistakably.

The dog joined the official Mitterand family as a plump little puppy ten years ago, and had his run of the elegant presidential quarters at the Palais de l'Elysée. When Baltique snuffled too intimately at visiting dignitaries — an issue often arising with politically powerful dogs — Mitterand would reproach him politely: "Monsieur Baltique, please behave and do not trouble my guests."

The best parts were their country walks — only the two of them — during holidays. Ended now for the master, and probably very soon for the grieving, elderly dog.

BASHAN — Short-haired German pointer (mostly, but as carefully indicated, not entirely pure); walking companion of Thomas Mann (1875 – 1955), esteemed German writer, Nobel Prize winner for literature in 1929. Bashan is the central figure in Mann's story, "A Man and His Dog" (*"Herr und Hund"* in the original German, where the dog's name appears as Bauschan).

"Bashan" is far from your simple dog story. Its 60 pages are thick with ambivalences and dichotomies, paradoxes and (for academics) antinomies: nature vs culture, the bourgeois vs the peasant, civilization vs solitude, psychic vs external forces, political allegories, multiplicity of viewpoints, and the symbolism of practically everything. In short, with all that emerges when wordy Teutonic weightiness takes the dog out for a pee.

The "Bashan" story first appeared in 1918. Mann was already famous, but the four years of WWI had, as he later explained, "paralysed my creative activities and driven me to a painful and exhaustive revision of all my spiritual fundamentals." The dog "idyll" was thus "my first creative effort, after long immersion in the task of self-examination and cultural critique."

Mann is famous for his epic novels: *Buddenbrooks* (1902), which traces the disintegration of a bourgeois family; *The Magic Mountain* (1924), which analyses the tensions of pre – WWI society; the biblical "Joseph" trilogy (1935 – 43); *Dr Faustus* (1947), which deals with the dark forces in German culture from which Nazism emerged. There are also scholarly essays, including one on Schopenhauer (*see* Atman) and shorter novels. As a recent academic critic has seen fit to note, Mann's novels are "tedious, but their tedium is sacred to us."

"Bashan" is not exactly tedious, but it is not gripping either; Steinbeck (*see* Charley) is by comparison a romp, and Virginia Woolf (*see* Flush) a happy read. Mann gives much description of the surroundings — natural and cultural — as he strolls and Bashan runs, often after birds and hares: valuable for the student who must write a paper.

Bashan was an unhappy, underfed puppy when he was adopted by the Mann family. Old, pure-bred collie Percy, suffering from a

Cover of recent German edition of A Man and His Dog, *commemorating author's 80th birthday.*

Zum 80. Geburtstag des Dichters
mit Zeichnungen von Gunter Böhmer
THOMAS MANN
Herr und Hund
FISCHER * BÜCHEREI

skin disease, had had to be shot. A puppy was available. But he was "an object that must have made any soul alive burst into half-pitying laughter":

Gaunt and knock-kneed, he stood there with his tail between his hind legs, his four paws planted together, his back arched, shaking. He may have been frightened, but one had the feeling that he had not enough on his bones to keep him warm; the poor little animal was a skeleton... He stood there expressive of nothing but wretchedness, stupidity, and a mute appeal for our forbearance. His hirsute appendages (a beard, a mustache, not right for a pointer) were then out of all proportion to his size and added a final touch of sour hypochondria...

But the Mann children were delighted. They had "lost their hearts to the wretched little quadruped under the table."

In vain we pretended to jeer at their lack of judgement and taste, feeling the pull at our own heartstrings. We saw that we should not be able to get him out of our heads; we asked ourselves what would become of him if we didn't take him. Into whose hands would he fall...?

So the puppy — then called Lux, subsequently Bashan — became part of the Mann family. He ran away once, was found again, then attached himself to the strongly authoritarian head of the family. Mann describes his hunting-dog's affinity to himself in terms of ultra-male supremacy:

This kind of dog can become a nuisance by always wanting to be with his master... It is a deep-lying patriarchal instinct in the dog, which leads him — at least in the more manly, outdoor breeds (*sic*) — to recognize and honour in the man of the house and head of the family his absolute master and overlord, protector of the hearth... whereas his attitude towards the rest of the family is much more independent...

In the family circle, he always sat at my feet, never by anyone else's...

But he became a nuisance to the master, bringing mud into the house, ruining the rug, and "smudging freshly written pages with his broad, hairy hunters' paws." So then the master's "fiat went forth that he might not be with me or in the house when I was there." Mann explains at some psychological length that "we can hardly speak of an independent existence carried on by Bashan when he is not at my side," even though, out in the garden, he may appear to be "playing with the children and putting on an absurd avuncular air . . ."

A few words about the Mann children, the ones who decided Bashan's fate, and about the Mann "family circle."

There were six children, brought up by Mann's beautiful wife Katia while father wrote his books. Two daughters killed themselves. When one of the sons attempted suicide, the father scolded him "because it disturbed his tranquillity." When a second attempt succeeded, Mann did not interrupt a lecture tour to attend his son's funeral.

(Could Mann's love for Bashan, such as it was, have been the most deeply felt?) When the dog died, Mann took the time to answer the many letters of condolence — including one from a dog, "Jack," who "wrote" to say how sorry he was.

Mann's daughter Erika had to give up her careers — dancer, journalist — to return to father when he needed her to manage his affairs. She was also briefly married to W. H. Auden, in what was apparently convenient for both: British citizenship for her, a cover for his homosexuality for him.

A scene in *Dr Faustus* is based on the suicide of a sister of Mann's. All in all, according to a review of the latest mammoth biography of Mann, the family "was so dysfunctional that it resembled a household from hell." But it was useful as it provided the raw material for his works.

As for the manly, patriarchal master, another message of this biography is that Mann was sexually attracted to handsome young men and that he "flirted with hotel waiters" as an elderly man: elements of homo-eroticism may be found in his stories. The *New York Times* review of this biography headlines Mann as "a heartless egocentric who engineered his own lionization." Even his well-known, explicitly stated anti-Nazism is called into question, in terms of "a latent hostility to Jews that he did not reveal to his Jewish wife, his ambivalence about the Nazis, and his anti-

Americanism" even while he was enjoying the best of lives in the best circles in America during the war.

None of this is even hinted at in the 1974 autobiography of Mann's wife Katia, written with son Michael's help. The tone is sunny and conversational, although personal likes and dislikes are made clear. Nothing about any family tragedies during her long, event-filled life, and hardly a hint of ambivalence — although the all-powerful husband was, by then, long dead.

Katia does say that her husband liked animals and that they liked him, but makes no mention of any dog in the household. Had she been jealous of Bashan? Wondered why he, and not she, was taken for walks?

Michael, the son who helped with this book, became a violinist (Mann loved music and researched it thoroughly for *Dr Faustus*). He joined the San Francisco Symphony, but gave it up for teaching German literature at Berkeley.

Michael's *Allegory and Parody in Thomas Mann's Idyll "A Man and His Dog"* (in German) was published in 1965 in a stupendously academic journal of German literature. His father would have been proud of its critical structure and academic tone. But the few readers familiar with the story might have wished for some (even repressed) dim memory of very young Michael present when the puppy Bashan was acquired "because of the children."

In his story, Thomas Mann emphasizes that Bashan was no intellectual. He was unlike his collie predecessor Percival, pedigreed, over-bred, and thus a "feeble-minded aristocrat." Mann is very good on the dangers of breeding for show. Bashan's parents were "both of good stock," but fortunately not of the same. Bashan's nature was simple and "peasant." He was happy

when all went well, which was no doubt for the best considering the dialectics spawning in Mann's mind whenever the two went walking.

An interesting post–Mann antinomy: the short-haired German pointer, Bashan's prevailing breed, rates 17th in "Obedience and Working Intelligence," as established in psychologist Stanley Coren's book. This is not at all bad — above the cocker spaniel and the Weimaraner, for instance. But curiously enough, the German *wire-haired* pointer ranks a far lower 44, down with the King Charles II's spaniels (*see* "Nell" and "Gwynne"), which Coren considers lovable but stupid. What fun Mann might have had on hair-smoothness as an obedience factor! (Note name of Esau, below.)

Other dogs appear in other stories by Mann. In "Felix Krull" (which has been considered an expression of Schopenhauer's philosophy of human identity) there is a joke about a Great Dane's unfortunate desire for a lapdog.

But his most unpleasant (and revealing?) dog story is the short "Tobias Mindernickel" (1897), about a lonely, shabby eccentric man, Tobias, whom all the children tease. (Have academic circles speculated a connection with Tobias [*see* Tobi] of the apocryphal book?) Tobias buys a puppy, names him Esau (Jacob's brother, in *Genesis*; the name means "hairy"). Tobias trains him incessantly, beats him, tells him how much he loves him. One day Tobias accidentally hurts Esau with a knife, then lovingly nurses him to health. But he becomes morose when the dog recovers and again becomes independent and playful.

The end, Mann says, is "too shocking, too inconceivable" to describe in detail. Tobias cuts a deep wound in the happy dog's chest, then embraces him: "My poor dog! How sad everything is. But I am with you, I will console you ..."

Two pages earlier, Tobias passionately holds Esau and says through his tears: "You see, you are my only ... my only ..."

Shades of Atman (q.v.). As Mann wrote in his 1938 essay on Schopenhauer, who greatly influenced him: "The actual world is the product of an arch-sinful, arch-stupid act of will."

BASKET — Intellectual poodle of writer Gertrude Stein (1874–1946). With her first real income from the publication in 1932 of *The Autobiography of Alice B. Toklas,* Gertrude Stein bought two elegant studded collars for Basket — plus a new eight-cylinder Ford, a made-to-order coat at Hermes, and a telephone.

An unusually well-connected poodle, Basket wagged his/her tail at most of the greats and soon-to-be-greats who visited Gertrude and Alice at their Paris home. It was a centre for writers and painters, who included Picasso (*see* Lump), Matisse, Gris, Hemingway, Sherwood Anderson, Clive Bell, André Gide, Paul Robeson, and many others.

Born in Philadelphia to a prosperous family, Stein spent her infancy in Vienna and Paris, and her childhood in Oakland, California, where she read Shakespeare as an eight-year-old. At Radcliffe, she studied psychology under William James, who said that young Gertrude was the "most brilliant woman student" he ever had. She also studied medicine, but had the independent means to go abroad and do as she liked.

Edmund Wilson wrote of her that she was "widely ridiculed and seldom enjoyed," but that she established important connections with other writers who became popular. Described as "vital, headstrong, cordial, with an insatiable appetite for people" — she was a good mix for a poodle person, but how unlike Schopenhauer (*see* Atman). She and her companion Alice, unlike popular conception of the two as total eccentrics, have also been described as "proper ladies and dedicated Republicans." However, when she was angry, she would swear: it happens in the best of circles. Her favourite song, which Basket must have known by heart, was "On the Trail of the Lonesome Pine."

Gertrude Stein's well-known, but not absolutely comprehended quotations — "a rose is a rose is a rose" and "pigeons in the grass alas" — are at least concise. Another fairly easy one is: "In the United States there is more space where nobody is than where anybody is. That is what makes America what it is."

Just before she died (in a little monologue attributed to more than one clear thinker), Gertrude Stein asked, "What is the

Gertrude Stein and Alice B. Toklas in the late 1920s.

answer?" No answer came. She laughed and said, "In that case, what is the question?"; and then she died.

BELLE AUDE — Belgian sheep dog, one of many dogs and cats loved and written about by Colette (1873 – 1954), French author known for her novels about youth, love, and animals; described as "a feminine Renoir of the pen."

Animals were an essential part of the life of Colette — born Sidonie-Gabrielle Claudine Colette Goudeket — but by no means a substitute for romantic love. She grew up "wild" in the country, the daughter of an army officer and a mother "of mixed blood." She married at 20, and her first husband, noticing her great imagination and talent for words, "collaborated" with her on four novels — the "Claudine" stories. A great success, they were attributed to him until the truth emerged.

Colette asserted her independence, divorced her husband, and became an actress and dancer: as always, her experiences became the material for her books. Those of this early period focused on the world of poor ballet dancers, but she also wrote *Seven Dialogues of Animals* in 1905.

Then came more romantic love: a second marriage, a second divorce. During WWI Colette became well-known as a journalist; to escape the barbarity of mankind, she published *Peace with Animals* in 1916.

By the Thirties she was famous for yet more novels, including the *Chéri* series. There was also *The Cat*, which tells of a young couple and the romantic triangle involving Saha, the cat: the bride is so nasty towards Saha that, in due course, the marriage ends.

Gigi, published in 1945, is probably Colette's best-known novel because it was made into a film starring the young Audrey Hepburn (who also knew all about dogs — two terriers — and a cat called "Tomorrow"). *Gigi* won the Oscar for the best film for 1958, four years after Colette's death.

On a visit to America, which she did not enjoy partly because she did not know any English, Colette happened to meet a dog on the street in New York. She stopped and stooped to chat with it, carrying on in her lilting, rapid French. When she had finished the conversation, she rose and said to her companion, "Finally, somebody in this country who understands French."

George Gordon Noel Byron, 6th Baron, in his romantic prime.

BOATSWAIN — Lord Byron's favourite dog, a Newfoundland. His grave is at Newstead (in Nottinghamshire, one of the family estates, near where Byron himself is buried) and the inscription on his monument tells the visitor, presumably in his master's words, that Boatswain had

Beauty without vanity, Strength without insolence, Courage without ferocity, and all the Virtues of man without his Vices.

The story of Byron's short, tumultuous, vivid life (1788 — 1824) is easily found. His poetry, although "much criticized on moral

grounds," was extremely popular and "exerted great influence on the Romantic movement." The public enjoyed Byron's constant attacks on hypocrisy, on "cant political, religious, and moral." The "Byronic hero" became a familiar figure, the term "Byronic" having come to mean contemptuous, rebellious of conventional morality: "proud, moody, cynical, defiant, implacable in revenge yet capable of deep affection."

Lord Byron died of fever in Greece, where he had gone to fight with the rebels, at the age of 34.

But what can we discover, without intensive research, about Boatswain? Byron's father, we learn with ease, was "profligate." What of Boatswain's sire? And of the dog's nature? Was he "Byronic"? As a Newfoundland, Boatswain was large and strong, active, probably heavier (110 to 150 pounds) than his master, and probably black. The breed is considered by some as "least likely to succeed as watchdog," together with other biggies such as the bloodhound, the St. Bernard, Irish wolfhound, and others.

In a throwaway line in her notes to *Flush* (q.v.), Virginia Woolf tells us that "some hold that Byron's dog went mad in sympathy with Byron," but alas, she gives no references. She does raise the issue of "the influence upon dogs of the poetry and philosophy of their masters." This, she adds, "deserves a fuller discussion than can here be given."

It is far easier to quote just a little from Byron:

> *Think you, if Laura had been Petrarch's wife,*
> *He would have written sonnets all his life?*

> *What men call gallantry, and gods adultery,*
> *Is much more common where the climate's sultry.*

> *There's not a joy the world can give*
> *Like that it takes away.*

> *Hatred is by far the longest pleasure:*
> *Men love in haste, but they detest at leisure.*

The last, as Byron knew, does not apply to dogs.

"BONNY" — Skye terrier favourite of Mary Stuart, Queen of Scots (1542 – 87). According to an eye-witness account, the small dog was present when Mary was beheaded by order of Elizabeth I of England, and added a poignant detail to the gory scene.

The history of Scotland, of its rulers, its aristocracy, and its common people, is a long train of plots, intrigues, rebellions, murders, massacres, gallantry, questionable documents, imprisonment; of religious conflicts (Protestant against Catholic), endless wars (about succession, about religion and power in general), of shifting international alliances and influences, of unproved charges and the usual lack of clear-cut evidence or historical "truth."

It has perhaps been written about more voluminously than similar (but of course, different) national independence movements. This may be partly because the Scots have for so long been literate as well as passionately devoted to their cause. The famous ballad, the "Skye Boat Song," about Bonnie Prince Charlie, the Young Pretender (who died about 200 years after Mary), was written by an author who lived in this century.

Here we shall deal only with the famous scene of Mary's execution, which was observed by scores of witnesses. What happened seems to have been that her little lapdog somehow managed to go with her mistress right to the execution block; Mary's women servants were no longer with her. After the much-described severing of the royal head, "Bonny" crept out from under the dead Queen's long petticoat and began to cry "beneath the severed head and the shoulders of the body."

Nobody could coax "Bonny" away. Finally, though, after the complex — and again much described — process of cleaning things up and disposing of evidence, Mary's faithful attendants washed the blood off the dog: it required several washings. But "Bonny" refused to eat, "and so pined away."

Based on a contemporary description, this follows the account in Lady Antonia Fraser's *Mary Queen of Scots*, a recent account of the Queen's life and death. (Mary, incidentally, was the great-great-grandmother of Prince Rupert [*see* Boy].)

Mary loved animals (except, presumably, the stags she hunted with her greyhound). She loved riding, and suffered when her long English imprisonment prevented it. In one of the "better" castles in England in which she was detained, she had as many as ten horses, her greyhound, and "the pleasure of little dogs."

"Bonny," as noted, has here been so named in honour of Bonnie Prince Charlie, great-great-grandson of Mary, who was defeated by the English forces on Culloden field in the Scottish Highlands in 1746.

Here is part of the "Skye Boat" ballad commemorating the Young Pretender (son of the Old Pretender who led an earlier, unsuccessful uprising) with all its "bonnies" (this Scots word comes from the Old French bon, and reflects France's influence on Scotland). The Island of Skye is, of course, Bonny's ancestral home:

> Speed, bonny boat, like a bird on the wing,
> "Onward" the sailors cry,
> Carry the lad that's born to be king
> Over the sea to Skye.

As for Mary, she comes out very well in accounts of her character and behaviour — except, of course, in contemporary Protestant statements. She is described as vigorous, attractive, intelligent, romantic, literary. She was married — badly — three times. The first, at 16, probably unconsummated, was to the sickly Dauphin of France who died soon after.

According to all accounts, she faced her long-awaited execution bravely and with dignity. Here is a contemporary jingle by a Scots patriot, which was attached to a piece of rope, the target being the hated Queen of England:

> To Jezebel that English whore,
> Receive this Scottish chain
> A presage of her great malheur
> For murdering our Queen.

Mary's dramatic, star-crossed story has been used by many

writers. The German dramatist, poet, and philosopher Friedrich Schiller, a great believer in the brotherhood of man and in revolt against tyranny, wrote a tragic play about Mary, with a fine confrontation scene between Mary and Elizabeth. The long dialogue, in iambic pentameter, showing two women in fatal conflict, makes rough going today; but the plot is all there for TV. One of the illustrations to the play, in an edition published in 1879, shows Mary wearing a large crucifix and with only one woman attendant. Imperious, unpleasant-looking Elizabeth, backed by several men and horses and holding a whip, has a whippet also in attendance. "Bonny" is still unborn.

BOY — Favourite dog of Prince Rupert (1619–82), who was known as the "Mad Cavalier."

Rupert was remarkable as a military hero, with interests in physics, chemistry, and art. He improved the process of mezzotint, and invented a type of brass called "prince's metal." Boy, no less unusual, became a focus of political dispute.

We are back in the tumultuous days of the Thirty Years War, which began the year before Rupert's birth: its ins and outs are impossible to follow here. It was also the time of the Great Rebellion in England — "Roundheads" (Parliamentarians) vs "Cavaliers" (Royalists). Rupert was outstandingly prominent in both sets of wars — courageously and sensibly (when the time came to change sides).

Born in Prague, he left for Holland with his family when his father was defeated. At the age of 14, he was with the Prince of Orange during a siege, and two years later served in the Prince's bodyguard. At 17, he visited England and entered Oxford "nominally." He was named, of all things, governor of a proposed British colony in Madagascar, "but this scheme fell through." King Charles had by now formed "a very high opinion of the young man's energy, talent, and resolution."

Rupert displayed "conspicuous bravery" during the continual wars but was captured and imprisoned at Linz in Austria in 1638, and held in "not very strict captivity" for three years. With Boy. Released, he became leader of the Royalist cavalry. With Boy. Became dominant figure of Royalist forces, exercising "bold and skillful strategy." With Boy.

But the defeat of the Royalists at Marston Moor in 1644 marked the end of this part of his career. And of Boy, who was killed in the thick of this decisive battle. It was usual for many horses to be killed in wartime, less so for dogs. The death of Boy at this famous battle "was greeted with exultation" by the victorious Puritans. The dog had been accused by the enemy of being his master's "familiar spirit" — an animal with the power of "divining" events. Boy also figured in pamphlets of the time.

CAESAR — White fox terrier of King Edward VII (1841 – 1910), son of Queen Victoria. Called "The Peacemaker" and "The most Edwardian of them all," this Edward ruled for only nine years, coming to the throne in 1901 at the age of 60 after a long career as a portly Prince of Wales.

His beloved Caesar, who has been called a dog "who could do no wrong" in a scrupulously detailed biography of Edward, had in effect his very own servant — the King's second footman who, besides cleaning Edward's shoes, also had the task of washing, combing, and feeding Caesar.

Whether Edward VII could, or could not, do "no wrong" is an interesting question today (*see* Harris). He loved the good life; in addition to dogs, this included heavy doses of eating and drinking and smoking, of women and racing and shooting. (This last was often a massacre of birds and deer, in the upper-class tradition.) His mistresses included great beauties and famous singers and actresses, and the friends he invited to accompany him while hunting or to provide sparkling conversation included some very rich Jews — most unusual for royalty. And he was involved, indirectly but in the public eye, in scandalous divorce cases.

Yet like his mother, although their styles were so different, he displayed "an iron resolve" to do his duty, and to cope with the new and often insoluble problems, foreign and domestic, facing Europe in this then new century. With all this, he was often depressed, and indeed bored with life as it was lived under his imperial mother.

Caesar was not the only royal dog. An earlier friend of Edward's, Jack, an Irish terrier, died in the summer of 1903, in the midst of an (appropriately) Irish crisis. Edward, said to be superstitious, noted impersonally in his private diary, in the third person: "The King's faithful Irish terrier 'Jack' dies suddenly at 11 p.m."

Edward's many two-legged friends also often caused him sorrow. He had been very fond of Prince Rudolf, the Austrian crown prince (*see* Shadow), and his suicide shocked Edward. Another old aristocratic friend, the superintendent of the royal stables (not the kennels) was discovered in a homosexual brothel. Edward, accused of many sins but not of this one, was scorching in his attack, noting that any man "addicted to such a filthy vice must be regarded as an unfortunate lunatic."

Yet Edward's eldest son, Prince Eddy, may well have been a homosexual — though he may well not have been "Jack the Ripper" as some have speculated, even to the extent that "Jack the Ripper" was a a pawn in a complicated royal cover-up of Eddy's homosexual doings. Feeble both mentally and physically, Eddy died at 27 before he could "desecrate" the throne, a "vacuous repository of the rumours he inspired." According to a new biography entitled *Prince Eddy and the Homosexual Underworld* — no less — the poor, sweet little Prince was ready to love anyone, man or woman, who approached him. The obvious cure, a sweet little fox terrier, apparently could not help him avoid his fate.

For Edward, the great consolation lay in his relationship with his younger son, who became George V. It was apparently ideal. They were more like brothers, as Edward once wrote to his son. And George, when his father died, wrote in his diary:

I have lost my best friend and the best of fathers. I never had a (harsh) word with him in my life. I am heartbroken and overwhelmed with grief.

Edward was a popular king. It was clear that the times were changing, and all was on public view: wrenching manœuvering between Tories and Liberals, between rich and poor, between Europe's various kingdoms, many of whose rulers were his relatives. The "German problem" was very present, and Edward's encounters with Bismarck (*see* Tyras) were marked by distrust.

(opposite) Prince looks to the side, terrier to the camera.

A song popular in the year before his death went, more or less:

There'll be no war
As long as there's a King like good King Edward,
For he hates that sort of thing!

Mothers needn't worry,
Peace with 'Onner
That's his motter
So God save the King!

As always, nobody knew what lay ahead; but people expected that things would now be worse. With Edward's death there was "a general sense as of an anchor slipping away," now that the country was bereft of "the familiar bulk that had stood between England and change." As one Edwardian put it, "I always felt that he somehow kept things together."

Vast crowds watched the London funeral procession on May 20, 1910. And here we return to Caesar, who was very visibly there. Carefully following protocol, and led on a leash by a kilted Highlander, Caesar, described as "disconsolate," walked right behind the gun-carriage that bore the coffin. And after Caesar came the German Emperor Wilhelm II, and then eight kings, and then a bevy of princes and princesses and heirs to other thrones, many of whom would soon vanish.

It was the last time a fox terrier would play such a visibly stellar role in such a crucial state event. (Fala's [q.v.] historically recorded bark at Franklin D. Roosevelt's funeral was hardly in the same category.)

After the terriers, themselves already down from the big hounds of absolute monarchs, the royal canines would soon descend another notch in breed size with the arrival of the corgis: a symbolic way of seeing the progress of royalty through history via their choice of breed.

CHARLEY — Elegant French-born blue poodle, travelling companion and hero of next-to-last book written by John Steinbeck (1902 – 68), popular American novelist, Nobel Prize winner (1962). Toby, an Irish setter, was an earlier dog of Steinbeck's, who was deeply attached to his dogs from childhood.

Charley, as an elderly poodle, was the hero of his book; Toby as a pup was a near-villain (but not really, in his owner's loving eyes) during the writing of *Of Mice and Men*. For Toby chewed up half of the only manuscript of the soon-to-be-famous novel when left alone one evening in 1936. Steinbeck wrote to his agent that this literary chew set him back months, as there was no other copy.

I was pretty mad, but the poor little fellow may have been acting critically. I didn't want to ruin a good dog for a manuscript I'm not sure is good at all. He got only an ordinary spanking.

The pup was following in the pawprints of other canine critics of famous works, while Steinbeck's reaction parallels the forgiving comments of Descartes (*see* Monsieur Grat) and Liebermann (*see* Pladumini).

Of Mice and Men was heralded as a best seller before it reached the bookstores. Steinbeck, suspicious of success but never of setters or poodles, wrote another note to his agent:

I wish I could be personally elated about all this fuss, but I can't. The book isn't that good . . . I'm still not sure Toby didn't know what he was doing when he ate the first draft. I have promoted Toby to be Lieutenant-Colonel in charge of literature.

As for the unpredictable literary enthusiasm of this country — I have little faith in it . . . I could defend myself against attack; I wish I were as sure I could defend myself against flattery.

Of Steinbeck's nearly 30 novels, perhaps the best known is *The Grapes of Wrath*, published in 1939 and filmed the next year. A story of the Great Depression, it tells of the wretched voyage of dispossessed farmers from the Oklahoma Dust Bowl to "golden" California, Steinbeck's native state. It continues to sell exceptionally well — about 50,000 copies a year, mostly, it must be admitted, to students; Steinbeck is still considered very "teachable."

Whatever the reason, his continuing posthumous success is amazing, with over 700,000 copies of most of his novels sold *every year*. Not bad for a writer described in his time as sentimental and derivative, "a well-meaning middlebrow" given to obvious symbolism, journalistic tricks, and so on.

He lived and drank and worked hard (and was, besides, a fascinated amateur marine biologist), and he was a crusader for social justice — although he attended Stanford University, not a poor boy's school. His output has been described as "eloquently partisan, filled with moral fervour and undismayed confidence in the integrity of the human spirit." But the "better" critics tended to place Steinbeck among the "second-rate and half-forgotten." Except for those sales, which must irritate them.

A 1995 biography of Steinbeck attempts to set the record straight and to show, in 536 pages, that Steinbeck got a "raw deal," that he was "quixotic, didactic, yet heroic," "unhappy, chronically uncertain, very gifted," a "turbulent individual and neglected paragon," and so on. A 1984 biography ran to no less than 1,116 pages. Steinbeck and his assorted dogs must be laughing all the way to the banks of Heaven.

During WWII, too old for active service, he chatted with President Roosevelt (*see* Fala) about possible schemes, and went overseas as a war correspondent: he found the experience too horrifying to put into a book. Instead he escaped to Hollywood and wrote the screenplay for *Lifeboat*, directed by Alfred Hitchcock (*see* Sarah), the story of survivors of a torpedoed passenger liner. "As the survivor of several battlefronts," one of his biographers commented, "he knew how they felt."

Travels with Charley is very different from the early books. It deals with a later and much changed, if still very problematical America, and is thus fascinating 30 years later still. The Bantam edition of *Travels with Charley*, subtitled *In Search of America*, from which these notes are taken (13th printing in six months,

National #1 Best Seller) radiates some high-class blurbs: "Loving, gentle, filled with wisdom"; "Trenchant observations about life." However, the *New York Herald Tribune* noted cautiously: "Unlike any other Steinbeck."

The "plot" is a trip in a van across America and back, made by Steinbeck, aged 60, with Charley, the object of constant monologues by Steinbeck. The van is named, surely too whimsically, "Rosinante." Steinbeck's wife — he married three times — stayed home.

Early in *Travels*, as he and his elderly poodle (bad hip, hit by a car when young) are setting off on their odd odyssey, Steinbeck gives this view of himself:

I have always lived violently, drunk hugely, eaten too much or not at all, slept around the clock or missed two nights of sleeping, worked too hard and too long in glory or slobbed for a time in utter laziness . . .

In my own life I am not willing to trade quality for quantity. If this projected journey should prove too much, then it was time to go

anyway. I see too many men delay their exits with a sickly, slow reluctance to leave the stage. It's bad theater as well as bad living.

We learn no less about Charley's character: that he had no nerves, and that unlike many dogs he was undisturbed by thunderstorms; that he loved travelling, and loved to get up early — and then go back to sleep after breakfast. For dog lovers, there are endless specific details: Charley's various techniques for waking Steinbeck up every morning. His cowardice, for which "he had developed a technique for concealing." His ailments — allergy, bladder problems. Encounters with a good vet and a bad vet.

Charley's behaviour and personality are interwoven with Steinbeck's views on America entering the Sixties. Charley's refusal to pee on a giant redwood, for instance, is embedded in a dissertation on the irreversible destruction of lumbering, and on geological time. And in a plastic-super-sanitized motel bathroom, in which Charley saves him from depression, Steinbeck notes: "A sad soul can kill you far more quickly than a germ."

And: "We have exchanged corpulence for starvation, and both will kill us." Bread has become "uniformly good and uniformly tasteless." And, 35 years ago: "Radio and TV are taking over the printed word."

Steinbeck was born to a typical conservative family in Monterey County, south of San Francisco, a heartland of Republicanism. "I might still be one if I had stayed there. President Harding stirred me toward the Democratic party and President Hoover cemented me there." But he hated Communism and, strangely, supported the Vietnam War.

On his travels with Charley, Steinbeck visited his Republican sisters in Monterey. They tried not to fight about politics, but it didn't work. They would soon be screaming at each other (no responses from Charley noted):

"John Kennedy was a so-and-so . . ."

"Well, if that's your attitude, how can you reconcile Dick Nixon?"

"Now, let's be calm . . ."

"Oh, how about the grocery in Santa Ana? How about Checkers (q.v.), my beauty?"

"Father would be turning in his grave if he could hear you . . ."

Steinbeck made a point of watching the violence and hatred during the early attempts at integration in New Orleans. He left Charley safely in the van elsewhere in the city and took a taxi to the daily "show," featuring one little Black girl escorted to school past ranks of jeering Whites.

It would be difficult to explain to a dog the good and moral purpose of a thousand humans gathered to curse one tiny human. I've seen a look in dogs' eyes, a quickly vanishing look of amazed contempt, and I am convinced that basically dogs think humans are nuts.

He noted several conversations with Southern White Supremacists; and then veered back to Charley, who "doesn't have our problems." The following is doubtless replete with various flaws found in Steinbeck: that his style was "hypermasculine sentimentality and Hemingwayesque *faux* simplicity," "crudely obvious symbolism and good liberal politics," etc. In any event, it takes us to Freud (*see* Jofi):

Charley doesn't belong to a species clever enough to split the atom, but not clever enough to live in peace with itself. He doesn't know about race, nor is he concerned with his sisters' marriages.

Quite the opposite, Steinbeck assures us. Because poor Charley once fell in love with a dachshund,

a romance racially unsuitable, physically ridiculous, and mechanically impossible. But all these problems Charley ignored. He loved deeply and tried dogfully.

And here is a practically psychoanalytical account of Charley after a traumatic near-encounter with a bear in a national park. Back in the van, Steinbeck, drink in hand, inspects the patient:

He was dazed. His eyes held a far-away look and he was totally exhausted, emotionally . . . He couldn't eat his dinner . . . (but) collapsed on the floor and went to sleep. In the night I heard him yapping, and when I turned on the light his feet were making running gestures and his body jerked and his eyes were wide open, but it was only a night bear.

I awakened him and gave him some water. This time he went to sleep and didn't stir all night. In the morning he was still tired. I wonder why we think the thoughts and emotions of animals are simple.

Here is another Charley dream, whose outward symptoms will be familiar to all dog owners. This time, he

had a dream so violent that he awakened me. His legs jerked in the motions of running, and he made little yipping cries. Perhaps he dreamed he chased some gigantic rabbit and couldn't quite catch it. Or maybe in his dream something chased him. On the second supposition, I put out my hand and awakened him, but the dream must have been strong. He muttered to himself and complained and drank half a bowl of water before he went back to sleep.

Finally, here is a scene in Chicago. To Charley's great annoyance, he had been left for three days in a kennel for grooming, while Steinbeck's wife flew in from the East for a brief meeting. After three days, husband said goodbye to wife and hello to poodle. That reunion is given in some detail:

Charley was torn three ways — with anger at me for leaving him, with gladness at the sight of (the van), and with pure pride in his appearance. For when Charley is groomed and clipped and washed, he is as pleased with himself as is a man with a good tailor or a woman newly patinaed by a beauty parlor, all of whom believe they are like that clear through.

Charley's combined columns of legs were noble things, his cap of silver blue fur was rakish, and he carried the pom-pom of his tail like the baton of a bandmaster. A wealth of combed and clipped mustache gave him the appearance and attitude of a French rake of the nineteenth century, and incidentally concealed his crooked front teeth . . .

If manners maketh man, then manner and grooming maketh poodle. He sat straight and nobly in the seat and he gave me to understand that while forgiveness was not impossible, I would have to work for it.

"He is a fraud," Steinbeck concludes this portion of the analysis (there is much more), "and I know it."

CHECKERS — Black-and-white cocker spaniel given to Richard Nixon's family during the 1952 presidential campaign, when Nixon (1913 – 94) was Dwight Eisenhower's running mate as Vice President on the Republican ticket. Checkers became a political issue during an election atmosphere of mud-slinging about gifts and campaign funds, and was the subject of a thoroughly reported and remembered speech by Nixon that came to be known as the "Checkers speech."

Born in California to a lower-middle-class Quaker family, Nixon will be remembered for his far-seeing foreign policy, but also as the only American president forced to resign while in office, as a result of the much publicized Watergate Affair of 1974.

A lawyer and navy veteran, and as a promising young politician with all the "right" virtues, Nixon first became prominent in the House of Representatives during the Forties in the Communist-hunting Un-American Activities Committee. Elected to the Senate in 1950, he became Eisenhower's running mate for two terms, and enjoyed the Republican landslide victories in 1952 — the "Checkers" year — and 1956.

But he did not enjoy Eisenhower's confidence or admiration. Much earlier in his life, Nixon's unhappy personality and his conviction that "nobody loves me" had already become apparent, as well as the contrast between the public and the private Nixon, and his concern for the "image" at the expense of all else.

When he was still "clean-cut" although already ambitious, this dichotomy was already clear to his sponsors, the owners of the strongly conservative, ultra-Republican *Los Angeles Times*. (It later "up-graded" itself and became more centrist.) At a party in prosperous Pasadena, California, in 1946, given by the "better people," among whom Nixon always felt an outsider, he arrived with his devout, anti-alcohol mother. Asked what she would drink, she said, "Milk." So did the Nixon men. Nixon took the hostess aside and asked for a straight bourbon, "but I don't want my mother to see me drinking it." The hostess, wife of the *Times* owner, decided that Nixon could indeed be used by her party, but could not be a friend.

The 1952 "Checkers speech" on television after the Republican convention was an attack on wealthy, well-born Democratic candidate Adlai Stevenson and his alleged acceptance of campaign gifts. In his preparatory notes for the speech, Nixon remembered how Franklin D. Roosevelt, in the bitter campaign against Thomas Dewey in 1944, had accused the Republicans of "attacking poor Fala (q.v.)." Well, he would use FDR's ploy; it "would irritate my opponents and delight my friends." He later told a friend, "I got a malicious pleasure out of it."

And so, in his "famous" but also "infamous" doggie remarks, Nixon began by saying that his family did indeed get a gift: somebody "down in Texas" had heard Pat say on the radio that the two little Nixon girls wanted a dog. And so along came this "gift," in a crate,

> ...and our little girl Tricia, the six-year-old, named it Checkers. And you know, the kids love the dog, and I just want to say this right now, that regardless of what they say about it, we're gonna keep it.

After the speech Nixon burst into tears, so moved was he by his own performance. It also saved his place on the ticket — Eisenhower never having been a fan — and greatly influenced the campaign.

After excellent media responses to the speech, Nixon's travelling press party became "euphoric." An aide had the bright idea of forming on the spot, in the plane, an "Order of the Hound's Tooth," with Checkers as mascot, Pat as president, membership cards, and "a small sliver of ivory symbolic of the clean tooth."

But as analysts have pointed out, "there were doubts about it later." Many resented that Nixon had made *himself* the issue rather than his politics. Even at the time, the entertainment weekly *Variety* made fun of him in two headlines on the "Checkers speech," echoing titles from two then-popular soap operas: "Just Plain Dick," and "Dick's Other Income."

The "Checkers speech" continued to surface among politicians. Eight years later, during Nixon's unsuccessful fight against John F. Kennedy, elderly Democratic speaker Sam Rayburn, a master of the old, pre—TV Senate style of wheeling and dealing, was watching candidate Nixon on TV (which would, in fact, hurt Nixon in the famous Kennedy debate: JFK was master of the medium without ever mentioning his dogs).

Rayburn simply could not bear watching Nixon's face. "Look what they're doing," he growled.

It's all going to be like that Checkers speech, trying to trick people into electing him. They're going to try and trick people into making him President.

But Rayburn was an ancient Democrat. A far worse and widely read public revelation was made by a prominent Republican, a friend of the Nixon family (and of Joe McCarthy, the best of credentials) who had campaigned for Nixon in 1952 — perhaps he had even patted Checkers — and again in 1956. This was Judge John J. Sirica, who presided over the Watergate hearings. In his book on the sad affair, Sirica wrote that after hearing the famous tapes and reading the (censored) transcripts, he "felt foolish" about having campaigned for Nixon:

At first, we were shocked by the frequent profanity. I came up the hard way, and the language was far from unfamiliar to me. But the shock, for me at least, was the contrast between the coarse, private Nixon speech and the utterly correct Nixon speech I had heard so often.

And Checkers himself? Did he, in the bosom of the Nixon family, become one of the few creatures who loved Dick boundlessly and showed his love daily? What language might Nixon have used if Checkers had, thoughtlessly, chewed a slipper?

And were there, back in 1952 among die-hard Republican dog lovers, any who wondered, listening to the speech, why this clean-cut young family man would not have already provided his little girls with their very own puppy? Even — just conceivably — by going to the local S.P.C.A., where even pure-bred doggies are available?

DEAR LOVE – Voltaire's mistress's little black dog. The "Divine Emilie," the Marquise du Chatelet (1706–49), was married to an understanding husband who primarily loved the army. When Voltaire (1694–1778) met Emilie, the mother of three children, she became his mistress and continued as such, with detours on both sides, for nearly 30 years. An outstanding intellectual and mathematician, Emilie was also the mistress of quite a few other Frenchmen, including the Duke of Richelieu; and as noted, of at least one little dog. This dog, a bitch, was in all probability called to her French supper by her French name, Cher Amour — appropriate to all aspects of this story, which has been marvellously recounted by Nancy Mitford.

Voltaire adored celebrities and loved being "In." His confessor said of him, when he was a boy, that "he had never known a child so devoured by a thirst for celebrity." By the time he was 30, Voltaire was France's most famous writer, busy with great names and "small" love affairs. He was also a smart business man and made a bundle through shrewd investments.

In 1733, Voltaire met Emilie, wife of a cavalry officer from a great French family. He was 39 and she was 27. He soon moved into a wing of her large isolated country house in Champagne. Emilie was devoted to study and learning, especially mathematics: she translated Newton and made an intensive study of Leibniz. She was also restless and unhappy. There were deceptions, and many scenes between her and Voltaire.

Many guests came to the château, some with their dogs. There were evenings of amateur theatricals, with plenty of off-stage scenes as well — "voluptuous disorder" with lots of flirtation, insults and reconciliations.

We know that Dear Love lived in splendidly aesthetic surroundings in Emilie's rooms, where she had her custom-made basket. The bedroom was panelled in yellow and blue, with an alcove for the bed which was covered in blue moiré; right next to it was Dear Love's basket, finished to match. Every dog should have a mistress (*sic*) with such an environment: paintings by Veronese and Watteau, a tiny boudoir, a dressing-room with a marble floor, armchair and two footstools upholstered in white taffeta, embroidered curtains, and naturally a terrace with a view.

One of the guests who came for a prolonged visit arrived with *her* dog (and maid), and here at least we know that it was a female, because detailed letters were written about this visit. This dog, whose name was Lise, alas came in heat, to the alarm of her mistress, who was sure that her maid would not take properly protective care of her. That is just what happened. Poor Lise

> was covered by one of those great mongrels in the farmyard, just as I had feared — now we'll have to see about an abortion, which may well have fatal results. I have never loved the poor little dog so much.

We do not know what happened to Lise; we know that Dear Love had puppies at least once, and that Emilie was far more concerned about them than about her own daughter: she was married off at the age of 16 to an old Duke, and her mother never saw her again.

Of all of Voltaire's involvements, Emilie was most jealous of the one with Frederick the Great, King of Prussia (*see* Alcmene). Emilie and Frederick fought complicated and high-class battles for the soul of Voltaire; she once said that she defied the King of Prussia to hate her more than she hated him.

Emilie became pregnant at the age of 44 by another lover, the Marquis de Saint Lambert. She and Voltaire returned from a trip; she played cards for 12 hours, and planned to finish her translation of Newton, but Voltaire noticed that Emilie was "low and obviously worried." He received the news "angelically" and was very concerned. She also notified her absent husband, with whom she had been on a "platonic" basis for 17 years. French society

had fun with this piece of gossip, and a joke made the rounds: Q: "Why does Mme du Chatelet suddenly want to see her husband?" A: "It is one of those cravings of pregnant women."

Emilie died soon after the birth of the baby, who also died. An evocative painting, described as "a posthumous fantasy of Voltaire and Emilie," shows the couple sitting under a tree in full 18th century dress, Emilie with a remarkable hat. It is really a kind of eternal triangle, because Dear Love is actively present, down at the right, her front paws on yards of billowing dress and her small nose nudging the Divine Emilie's bracelet.

The dog's profile, it might be said, bears a remarkable resemblance to that of "Zodi" (q.v.) and looks quite attractive. But she is spotted and not black; does a "posthumous fantasy" imply idealization? The two lovers may also have been idealized in the painting. Emilie as a young woman, at least according to one catty female's report, was not much to look at: "thin, dry, flat-chested, huge arms and legs, huge feet, tiny head, tiny little sea-green eyes, bad teeth, black hair, a weather-beaten complexion, vain, overdressed, untidy." (To be Divine, study your Newton.) On the other hand, most of Voltaire's men friends were attracted by her; one spoke of "her beautiful big soft eyes, her noble, witty and piquant expression."

In 1741, when he was 46, Voltaire had told Emilie that he was now too old to make love: "The heart does not age, but this immortal is condemned to live in a ruin." At the same time, he was writing love letters to his young niece, Louise, recently widowed. After Emilie's death, Voltaire moved to his niece's home ("you are my one consolation, the only hope of my life") and lived with her until his death 29 years later. There were no children.

Emilie's son was guillotined during the Revolution, and her grandson died in prison. The family was extinct.

But perhaps Dear Love's distant descendants are frisking about the old territory in Champagne, where their many-times-great-grandmother knew Voltaire.

DELORES — Maltese terrier bitch, one of the many dogs, cats, and birds who lived on intimate terms with actress Tallulah Bankhead (1903 – 68).

Unpredictable, imperious, and uninhibited, to put it mildly, the sexy, husky-voiced star of stage and screen possessed a personality that permitted few human friends at close range. Instead, she kept a "zoo" in her New York hotel, and her huge capacity for love was centred on her animals.

Although Tallulah came from a top-ranking American family (her uncle was U.S. Senator from Alaska, her Congressman father was Speaker of the House from 1936 to 1940), she enjoyed being quoted for quips such as "I'm pure as the driven slush."

A close glimpse of Tallulah and her dogs (and cats) is provided by the remarkable vet, Dr Louis Camuti, who made house calls to selected animals and their owners, and thus could judge human and animal behaviour from an unusual viewpoint. Tallulah, Camuti makes clear, was very hard on herself and on everyone who came near her: it was her pets that were pampered and received the best of herself.

At the time that Tallulah was preparing for her role in *A Streetcar Named Desire*, Delores was neutered by Dr Camuti, as he had done earlier for Gabrielle, the peke. The doctor then arrived at the hotel a few days later to remove the stitches. He expected dramatic scenes and tensions, and was not disappointed.

Additional scenes and tempests blazed around, of all things, Delores's tranquillizers when she accompanied Tallulah by plane for appearances. On one occasion, the actress telephoned Camuti from Hollywood to say that the dose had been too small, and that the good doctor should send more pills from New York to Hollywood. But you can get the pills in Hollywood, Camuti suggested reasonably.

"Send them!" roared Tallulah.

But that's ridiculous, said Camuti. Tallulah banged down the receiver.

A moment later the doctor's telephone rang again.

Tallulah: "You'll send them?"

"No." Bang goes the phone.

Ten minutes later, the phone rang again, and Camuti knew just about what to expect. "Somebody will come by your home very soon to collect my dog's pills," said the famous husky voice.

On another occasion, Tallulah made a marvellous scene at the airport, on her way to Las Vegas with Delores, when the airport manager said she could not possibly take Delores's huge travelling case on board, and that the airline would give her a smaller one. Dr Camuti, present at the airport in order to give Delores her tranquillizing injection at the last moment, watched the proceedings with amazement.

"Listen to me, young man," said the actress acting out her scene. "Delores goes in her own case."

The manager was called. A crowd gathered. Also enjoying the spectacle were the members of Tallulah's entourage who were going along — Delores's attendant, Tallulah's lawyer, her hairdresser, her cosmetician, her maid, and possibly most astounding, her dentist. But the centre of the hullabaloo was Delores.

Dr Camuti finally took the top manager aside, explained that the dog would sleep quietly all the way, and that allowing Tallulah to take the large case into her compartment was the only way to assure a tranquil flight. And so it was.

Tallulah once told Dr Camuti that she could not endure being alone: "When I go to the toilet, I need somebody along to hold my hand." But as noted, for humans to be with her was like being "at the center of a hurricane . . . but love was the measure of her soul, and that her animals knew."

EIKO VON BLUTENBERG and ROBINSON — Dachshunds of Dorothy Parker, née Rothschild (1893 – 1967), American writer of short stories and verse known for her caustic wit and sarcastic, cynical view of the human condition. Parker's personal life reflected her literary output. Hers was not a happy one, especially in the relations between men and women, which had suddenly become liberated during the Roaring Twenties.

Born in New Jersey to a Jewish father and a Scotch mother, she was educated in, of all places, a convent and was expelled for writing a very unacceptable essay. Young Dorothy began to work in New York, first at *Vogue* (fashion captions), and then at *Vanity Fair*, where intellectual writers congregated for witty talk, and for lots of liquor at mostly liquid luncheons.

She married her first husband, handsome Edwin Pond Parker, in 1917 when he was an officer in WWI; they were divorced in 1928. She fell in love with three more men, suffered, wrote, confided in her dogs, and finally married Alan Campbell in 1933. But no bed was ever one of roses:

> *Here's my strength and my weakness, gents,*
> *I loved them until they loved me.*

Or:

> *By the time you swear you're his,*
> *Shivering and sighing,*
> *And he vows his passion is*
> *Infinite, undying —*
> *Lady, make a note of this:*
> *One of you is lying.*

None of these lyrics on the impossibility of love apply to Parker's relationship with her dachshunds. She loved them all her life; but although faithful in her fashion to dachshunds, she also had a Scottish terrier called Daisy, a boxer called Flic, a Dandie Dinmont terrier called Timothy, a Bedlington called Wolf, and a Boston terrier named, for some reason, Woodrow Wilson.

And yet: are we to interpret some unrequited aspect to the dachshund's soul in Steichen's 1932 photograph of the pair? Dorothy sits and smiles sweetly to one side, wearing one of her famous hats, hands demurely in a muff. Eiko von Blutenberg (unless it was Robinson) stares pointedly off in the other direction!

During the Thirties her reputation for witticisms was constantly increasing, though many attributed to her were not hers. But that was how it was at the famous "Round Table" of the Hotel Algonquin, where the wits gathered.

Always concerned for the underdog, Parker became involved in serious social problems — justice, international politics, and especially the Spanish Civil War. She visited Spain in 1937 and on her return worked with great emotion for the Loyalist cause and against the Fascists, a commitment that brought accusations of Communism.

It was a double life. The year after the visit to Spain, she and her husband wrote the saccharine script for *Sweethearts* with Nelson Eddy and Jeanette MacDonald; they had also done *A Star is Born*, but the only one they were proud of was Lillian Hellman's *The Little Foxes*.

In her acid comments, Parker did not even spare fellow dog lovers. One of her famous barbs pierced Katherine Hepburn (*see* Lobo) in an early play: "She ran the whole gamut of emotions from A to B."

And on being told that ex-President Calvin Coolidge (*see* Rob Roy) had died: "Why, I never even knew that he was alive."

To bring to our present day the way Dorothy Parker viewed things over half a century ago: "If all the young ladies who attended the Yale promenade dance were laid end to end, no one would be the least surprised."

"ELOISE" — Mixed-breed dog who lived with French philosopher Jean Jacques Rousseau (1712–78). There was also a cat, and the three shared a cottage at the village of Montmorency where Rousseau wrote his didactic novel *La Nouvelle Eloise* in 1756. Considered immoral, it naturally created a furore so we could call the dog "Eloise." A few years later his novel *Emile, ou Traité de l'Education*, dealing with education, appeared.

Quarrelsome (except with his animals), sentimental, always unorthodox, Rousseau became an idol of the French Revolution, which began ten years after his death. He is remembered for his "Back to Nature" philosophy — that civilization has corrupted man, that progress is an instrument of oppression, that "savage" man is superior to the "civilized":

The greater part of our ills are of our own making, and . . . we might have avoided them nearly all by adhering to that simple, uniform, and solitary manner of life which nature prescribed.

Actually, his own life was marked by constant quarrels, paranoia, ill health, perversity, questionable sincerity, and so on. At the age of ten, sent to live with a pastor "to learn Latin and all that twaddle," he was punished by being beaten by the pastor's unmarried sister. In his autobiographical *Confessions* he described his pleasure at the episode, seen as "a fitting prologue to a life of masochism":

I found the experience less dreadful in fact than in anticipation, and the very strange thing was that this punishment increased my affection for the inflicter. It required all the strength of my devotion and natural gentleness to prevent my deliberately earning another beating. I had discovered in the shame and pain of the punishment an admixture of sensuality which left me rather eager for a repetition by the same hand.

His early life was a series of subterranean adventures, patrons, liaisons, and inconclusive attempts at music and teaching. Fame and famous friends came when he was in his thirties; the quarrels continued.

Towards the end of his life, Rousseau married his mistress; the ceremony was "after a fashion, and of his own devising." This "wife," a servant at an inn, has been described by later biographers as having "little beauty, no education or understanding, few charms, and a detestable mother."

Five children were born of this union, as Rousseau states in his autobiography. All were deposited at birth at the Foundlings' Hospital, thus

> safeguarding them from their father's fate, and from that which would have overtaken them at the moment when I should have been compelled to abandon them... I am sure that they would have been led to hate, and perhaps to betray, their parents. It is a hundred times better that they had never known them.

There are those who suggest that Rousseau simply "made up" his offspring to refute rumours of impotence. Yet he considered himself an expert on child-rearing. His *Emile*, or *Education* advises mothers to breast-feed their children, and it became a guide

to modern theorists of education, such as John Dewey and the "Progressive" movement, which opposed the old rigid "classical" education.

Romantic and revolutionary, Rousseau was of course strongly against the monarchy. So was Voltaire, with whom he corresponded. But Voltaire and the liberal rationalists believed that the human condition could be improved slowly, by reason and not violently and by "instinct," as Rousseau believed.

When Rousseau sent Voltaire his publication on Inequality, Voltaire thanked him for his work and its thesis that society could be cured by returning to nature — to man and animals in the wilderness. But, Voltaire wrote, "Nobody has so spiritedly attempted to turn us into animals":

Reading your book awakes in one the feeling that one ought to run around on all fours. But since I gave up this activity 60 years ago, I unfortunately do not feel in the position to take it up again.

Of Rousseau, Voltaire wrote to a friend that "this Jean Jacques Rousseau resembles a philosopher about as much as an ape resembles a man"; he is "Diogenes' dog gone mad." Yet Voltaire, true to his principles, defended Rousseau against his enemies, and even invited him to stay with him when he was in danger. Both men were revered by the activists of the French Revolution; the revolutionaries moved the remains of both men to the Pantheon in Paris.

The lithograph of Rousseau at Montmorency shows the little dog looking somewhat apprehensive. The cat seems comfortable (or, possibly, ready to leap) in the lap of the philosopher, who in turn appears distinctly at peace with his four-legged friends. Rousseau had moved to this cottage (and five years' free lodging), which belonged to the Marshal of Luxembourg, after "moving out in a huff" from his previous idyllic residence in the same village following a quarrel with his patroness.

With all this, Rousseau's influence is considered "unrivalled in literary history," his defects redeemed by "the passionate sincerity of even his insincere passages."

FALA — Scottish terrier, constant companion of Franklin Delano Roosevelt (1882 – 1945), 32nd President of the United States. Fala was the first modern media dog; he was known to millions of radio-listening Americans because his master was the first presidential master of the media — the first, and possibly the greatest.

Roosevelt's weekly radio talks to the nation during the Thirties and Forties, in which he used to put across his political programmes, were a national event in those pre – TV, historically decisive days. The "fireside chats" were conversational, easy, personal, warm, casual-sounding — and very carefully worked out. Roosevelt had earlier practised the infant art of being believable for mass consumption when he was Governor of New York in the Twenties, when radio was just getting started.

As President, FDR spoke to his "fellow Americans" about his wife, his children, his dog. As one admiring and knowledgeable observer of the media's role in politics evaluated one of the "Fala Events":

Some 35 years later, an astonishing number of Americans who did not remember the names of the dogs of Harry Truman, Dwight Eisenhower, and John Kennedy, remembered the name of Franklin Roosevelt's dog because he had spoken with them about Fala, "my little dog Fala," about Fala's Irish being up over Republican criticism. It was an awesome display of (media) mastery.

Irish indeed! It was a typical Roosevelt joke, and he loved them. Fala was undiluted Scotch, whose ancestors came from the Highlands and whose progeny was very popular in America. The low-slung "Scottie" is one of the earliest of the terriers indigenous

to Scotland; usually black, it may also be grey or wheaten. It is related to the West Highland terrier, which is always white, and to the Sealyham (which was developed in Wales). The Scottie, active and short-legged, was used for routing foxes and rodents — and in Roosevelt's day, Republicans.

For those too young to remember the Golden Age of Radio, of Roosevelt, and of Fala: FDR was both hugely loved and hugely hated. Born to a wealthy family — no wonder the Republicans attacked him for his social welfare programmes — his European travel began when he was three. He spoke fluent French and German, and of course went to the best schools. His boyhood was busy with hunting, shooting, polo, and tennis. He graduated from Harvard in 1904 and then from Columbia Law School.

In 1906 he married a sixth cousin, Eleanor Roosevelt. President Theodore Roosevelt attended the ceremony; he was an uncle of the bride and fifth cousin of the groom. The marriage was not known for romantic warmth, and the children, rather like those of his friend-to-be Winston Churchill (*see* Rufus) never reached their parents' stature. Eleanor became an internationally known personality in her own right.

After a round of business, philanthropic, and social activities, Roosevelt became interested in politics under the influence of his distinguished relative, Theodore Roosevelt. He became New York State Senator with a reputation for "progressiveness and independence," then Assistant Secretary of the Navy.

And then, in 1921, he was stricken by polio, and emerged paralysed from the waist down. He worked and exercised long and hard, but recovery was only partial. He was never able to walk unassisted, and was always photographed seated — later, with Fala down there at his ankle. Roosevelt headed the Boy Scouts Foundation of America, raised large sums of money, and set up a non-profit hydrotherapeutic centre for other polio victims.

In 1929, in spite of his serious physical disability, he was elected Governor of New York, and in 1932 became the Democratic presidential candidate, considered to be in the happy position of being able to unite the discordant Democratic elements.

His inauguration in 1933 took place as the nation was in "the throes of a crisis unprecendented in time of peace" — the Great Depression; and at the same time, the rise of Adolf Hitler. America seemed "at the brink of an abyss." FDR's eloquent inaugural address caught the popular imagination, and thus began what has been described as "the most daring Presidential leadership in American history." FDR was the only President ever to be elected to four terms.

Fala came into the President's life the year before he and Churchill met for the first time. This was on their super-secret rendezvous on a battleship in mid-Atlantic in 1941, where the two leaders drew up the "Atlantic Charter." This places Fala in geopolitical history.

To place him in FDR's private life: the little Scottie arrived in August 1940 as a gift from an admiring woman friend of FDR's, Margaret Suckley, and was named by the President. When Margaret died, at nearly 100, in 1991, a journal of thousands of pages was found, with many new details on FDR's life. Margaret (like Eleanor, she was also a Roosevelt relative, a sixth cousin once removed) was one of the many "amiable" women with whom Roosevelt liked to gossip, joke, and relax. Margaret greatly respected Eleanor, but observed in her journal that she was "lacking in only one thing, and that is the ability to relax and *play* with him."

This is something that any little terrier is well equipped to do, and although Margaret was certainly not always with FDR — they took some fascinating trips together and were in constant touch by letter and telephone — Fala was in fact nearly his closest companion. Indeed, it was a very bright idea on her part: a loving, unmarried, and adoring woman can do worse than give the object of her affections a little dog who will always be at his side and will be immortalized in photographs — thanks to her.

Six years before Fala arrived at the White House, Churchill wrote an admiring essay about America's controversial President, entitled "Roosevelt from Afar," when their remarkable cooperation during WWII was still in the future. Here is Churchill, born to the British purple yet, like rich Roosevelt, concerned for "the common man" writing in 1934 about his still unmet friend. Roosevelt, Churchill wrote,

is an explorer who has embarked on a voyage as uncertain as that of Columbus, and upon a quest which might conceivably be as important as the discovery of the New World.

Concentrating on the Depression, Churchill concluded his evaluation:

It is certain that Franklin Roosevelt will rank among the greatest of men who have occupied (the presidency). His generous sympathy for the underdog, his intense desire for a nearer approach to social justice . . . his composure combined with activity in time of crisis, class him with famous men of action . . .

After their meeting on the battleship in 1941, Roosevelt wrote to Margaret of the first impression made by Churchill: "He is a tremendously vital person and in many ways is an English Mayor LaGuardia."

Roosevelt to Churchill, in answer to congratulations on his 60th birthday in 1942, with the war at its dismal first stage:

"It is fun to be in the same decade with you."

And as Fala would have wished to communicate to Rufus: "What marvellous masters we had! Their problems were enormous, but we were always there!"

Rufus to Fala: "Was ever a poodle, a Scottie so lucky!"

When FDR died on April 12, 1945, an editorial in the American press noted that, in response to the guns fired over the President's grave, those present could hear "Fala's sharp answering bark."

FLUSH — Golden-red cocker spaniel beloved by poet Elizabeth Barrett (1806 – 61). When she was 40, and after several years of loving only Flush, EB eloped to marry poet Robert Browning (1812 – 89) in 1846, escaping from her autocratic Victorian father's London house. She ran off with only Flush and her personal maid to live in romantic Italy. (For the conflicting emotions of the man-woman-dog triangle, *see also* Nero, Pet.)

Before meeting debonair Robert Browning, six years her junior, the sickly Elizabeth, usually restricted to her bedroom, books, and writing (she had read Homer in Greek at eight) was well known in literary London, but loved only Flush. One sad day she wrote a sonnet to the dog. Here is a slightly shortened version — for who today has time for iambic pentameter dedicated to a spaniel conceived as pagan Pan? Elizabeth, recalling a good cry on her sofa:

> *You see this dog. It was but yesterday*
> *I mused forgetful of his presence here . . .*
> *When from the pillow, where wet-cheeked I lay,*
> *A head as hairy as Faunus thrust its way*
> *Right sudden against my face — two golden-clear*
> *Great eyes astonished mine, — a drooping ear*
> *Did flap me on either cheek to dry the spray!*
> *I started first, as some Arcadian,*
> *Amazed by goatly god in twilight grove . . .*
> *My tears off, I knew Flush, and rose above*
> *Surprise and sadness — thanking the true Pan,*
> *Who, by low creatures, leads to heights of love.*

Flush (c.1842 – 53) was for decades a very famous dog. He was probably known to more VIP's and readers of literature even than Millie (q.v.), thanks to Virginia Woolf's remarkable biography *Flush*, published in 1933. Judged by sheer quantity of mass recognition, modern Millie of course wins out, what with popular magazines and today's media coverage. But Barbara Bush is no Virginia Woolf, who decided to make the literary experiment of writing about a dog as a central character in a real biography —

(above left) Young Robert Browning.

(above) Elizabeth Barrett, now happily Mrs Robert Browning.

(left) Flush at home on the sofa.

not an "autobiography," and not in the first person. Three years before *Flush* was published, a very successful play, *The Barretts of Wimpole Street*, by Rudolf Besier, opened in London, with a cocker spaniel right on stage for all to see; it later also became a film.

Years later, Flush was still appearing — in of all things, scholarly inquiries into the nature of "personality and impersonality" in the modern novel. As an American professor wrote in 1978 of Virginia Woolf's biography, Flush is an "independent projection of EB's physical being:

Elizabeth is prudish, Flush is a father while scarcely out of puppyhood; Elizabeth is restrained, Flush spontaneous; Elizabeth can write and speak, Flush is illiterate. But this inability is his great strength; since his brain is not smothered in cerebral cortex Flush can see the real light, touch his paws to an earth that is moister, more tangible, than any ever felt by human foot.

In true academic earnestness, the professor continues:

The human mind and the human nose are alike gross and incompetent in their categorization: the mindless animal perceives the plenitide of things . . . The dialectic of the aesthete and the realist here reaches its point of maximum spread: while Elizabeth Barrett explores the most delicate refinements of unreality, Flush is the unconceiving and inconceivable realist . . .

And after several quotations from *Flush*:

Language has despoiled the world and laid human experience in waste . . . Dogs know their small territory better than any man will ever know anything . . .

Flush was a gift to Elizabeth from her friend Miss Mary Russell Mitford, also a writer and also sired by a nasty Victorian father; she has her own entry in Literature Encyclopaedias. (*See* Dear Love for a literary family connection.) Miss Mitford's father raised greyhounds and cocker spaniels; but the family had become poor because he wasted all his daughter's earnings. Miss Mitford could have sold nicely pedigreed Flush, the beautiful young puppy who so adored going for walks with her in the countryside (and was much better "bred" than Mr Mitford, as Virginia Woolf is quick to assure us). Ten or 15 pounds could be had for him, an enormous help. But

to sell Flush was unthinkable. He was of the rare order of objects that cannot be associated with money . . . a fitting token of the disinterestedness of friendship (that) may be offered to a friend who is more like a daughter, to a friend who lies secluded . . . in a back bedroom in Wimpole Street, a friend who is no other than England's foremost poetess . . . Yes, Flush was worthy of Miss Barrett; Miss Barrett was worthy of Flush.

Dear Miss Mitford decides that the "great sacrifice must be made," and walks with Flush to the house on Wimpole Street. Virginia Woolf makes the scene poignant — from Flush's point of view. He has never been in a grand house, he believes Miss Mitford has deserted him, and after considerable anguish, unknown rooms, staircases, panic, despair, he finally hears a voice say, "Flush." Twice.

He had thought himself alone. He turned. Was there something alive in the room with him? Was there something on the sofa?

In the wild hope that this being, whatever it was, might open the door; that he might still rush after Miss Mitford and find her — that this was some game such as they used to play at home — Flush darted to the sofa.

"Oh, Flush!" said Miss Barrett, looking him in the face for the first time; and for the first time, Flush looked at her.

Each was surprised. Heavy curls hung down on either side of Miss Barrett's face; large bright eyes shone out; a large mouth smiled. Heavy ears hung down on either side of Flush's face; his eyes, too, were large and bright: his mouth was wide. There was a likeness between them. As they gazed at each other each felt: Here am I — and then each felt: But how different!

Hers was the pale worn face of an invalid, cut off from air, light, freedom. His was the warm ruddy face of a young animal; instinct with health and energy.

Broken assunder, yet made in the same mould, could it be that each completed what was dormant in the other?... But no. Between them lay the widest gulf that can separate one being from another. She spoke. He was dumb. She was woman; he was dog. Thus closely united, thus immensely divided, they gazed at each other. Then with one bound Flush sprang on to the sofa and laid himself where he was to lie for ever after — on the rug at Miss Barrett's feet.

However great the temptation, we cannot continue to quote at length from this wonderful work. It is, after all, a whole little book — 163 pages, complete with notes, and opening with a short account of the origin of the spaniel breed. A supremely accredited academic research expert (Daniel J. Boorstin) assured us as recently as 1992 that "Virginia Woolf was not a dog lover," but that "she liked to imagine herself as an animal — a goat, a monkey, a bird, and now a dog, and then wonder what this would have done to herself." Perhaps. Certain only is that Virginia Woolf — very unlike Elizabeth Barrett — had recurring bouts of madness, and that in 1941 she committed suicide by drowning, leaving two letters. One was to her husband Leonard, the other to her sister Vanessa Bell, whose drawings of Flush and Elizabeth are the end-pages of the book.

Briefly, then: there are two dramatic events in this biography, in addition to the careful analyses of daily moods. One is the kidnapping of Flush by a gang from the slums near the wealthy Wimpole home. Snatching, for ransom, well-known, well-bred dogs running loose was a source of income in London 150 years ago. The worried owners would receive a note saying, "Pay up or you'll get your dog's head in a paper bag." Flush was kidnapped three times. And totally traumatised.

The second emotional drama centred, naturally, on the appearance of Robert Browning, the "other man" in Flush's hitherto exclusive relationship with Elizabeth. Virginia Woolf describes in detail Robert's courtship, Elizabeth's return to "life," and Flush's hatred of his rival:

(opposite) Elizabeth in Italy, Flush snoozing in an Italian market.

Sleep became impossible while that man was there. Flush lay with his eyes wide open, listening. Though he could make no sense of the little words that hurtled over his head from two-thirty to four-thirty three times a week, he could detect with terrible accuracy that the tone of (Elizabeth's) words was changing . . . (from) forced and unnaturally lively at first, to a warmth and an ease that he had never heard in it before.

Each time the enemy arrived, changes took place in their voices, new and ominous sounds:

Now they made a grotesque chattering, now they skimmed over him like birds flying widely; now they cooed and clucked . . . then Miss Barrett's voice went soaring and circling in the air; and then Mr Browning's voice barked out its sharp harsh clapper of laughter; and then there was only a murmur . . .

They hardly noticed Flush. He might have been

a log of wood lying there at Miss Barrett's feet for all the attention Mr Browning paid him. Sometimes he scrubbed his head in a brisk, spasmodic way, energetically, without sentiment . . . Flush felt nothing but an intense dislike for Mr Browning. The very sight of him, so well tailored, so tight, so muscular, screwing his yellow gloves in his hand, set his teeth on edge. Oh! to let them meet sharply, completely in the stuff of his trousers! And yet; he dared not . . .

But in the end he does dare, and bites Mr Browning, and . . . But the reader is urged to track down a copy of the book, which contains as it does the most complete experiment of its kind, the most complete attempt to uncover the dog's view of its relationship with its owner. And, of course, there are Flush's adventures in Italy, and his fleas; the arrival of a baby Browning; and finally, Flush's death.

But let us maintain a sense of proportion, and close with some of Elizabeth's most famous lines — from her *Sonnets from the Portuguese*, written not to Flush but to Robert. The sonnet form, in the words of a critic, "restricted her tendency to prolixity" and thus helped form her best work:

> *How do I love thee? Let me count the ways.*
> *I love thee to the depth and breadth and height*
> *My soul can reach, when feeling out of sight*
> *For the ends of Being and ideal Grace . . .*

And from Robert's vast output, just two lines from *The Ring and the Book*:

> *Vows can't change nature, priests are only men,*
> *And love likes stratagem and subterfuge . . .*

GEIST — One of three dachshunds belonging to Matthew Arnold (1822 – 88), renowned Victorian poet, prolific prose writer, and educational inspector. Arnold was more or less contemporary with Schopenhauer; and *Geist*, in German, means "spirit, soul," possibly somewhat akin to Atman (q.v.). Arnold, however, preferred defining Geist as "intelligence."

Strictly speaking, Geist belonged to one of Arnold's sons who had gone to Australia. As so often happens, the little dog was left in the parents' care, and died at home in the family circle. Arnold's other two dachshunds had less spiritual names — Kaiser and Max.

Arnold had the finest English education. His father was the great headmaster of Rugby; the son won prizes at Oxford, and later dedicated his life to education as much as to literature. To earn a living when he married, Arnold accepted an appointment as Inspector of Schools. After being sent to the continent to observe education there, he submitted unusually thorough reports whose purpose was to convince the English people that education ought to be a "national concern." His message was always "Organize your secondary education."

His critical essays ranged from "Culture and Anarchy" to "St Paul and Protestantism," "Literature and Dogma," "Irish Essays," and on and on. His most famous poems include "The Forsaken Merman," "Empedocles on Etna," and "The Scholar-Gypsy." Many were memorials to departed friends, including the poem called "Geist's Grave," when the dachshund died.

His description of Oxford, where he was Professor of Poetry for ten years, is typical of Arnold's stately prose, his "classical austerity" (and his concern for commas):

That home of lost causes, and forsaken beliefs, and unpopular names, and impossible loyalties.

In memory of Geist, then, and of a once famous writer, here are the concluding lines of "Dover Beach," written over a hundred years ago. It is a safe bet that nothing more romantic or more contemporary will be written between now and the next millennium:

> *Ah love, let us be true*
> *To one another! for the world, which seems*
> *To lie before us like a land of dreams,*
> *So various, so beautiful, so new,*
> *Hath really neither joy, nor love, nor light,*
> *Nor certitude nor peace, nor help for pain;*
> *And we are here as on a darkling plain*
> *Swept with confused alarms of struggle and flight,*
> *Where ignorant armies clash by night.*

And yet — perhaps Geist's master, and Geist's spirit, are not so forgotten after all. "Dover Beach" cropped up during the confused alarms of America in the 1960s and 1970s when no less than Philip Roth was describing certain upbeat aspects of the American literary scene. Some novels were, he wrote, "as though 'Dover Beach' ended happily for Matthew Arnold, and for us, with the poet standing at the window with a woman who understands him." (Or with a dachshund.)

Later still, already well into what is called post–modernism, Joseph Epstein wrote a definitive evaluation of Arnold in 1982. After giving due space to Arnold's critics, including T. S. Eliot who disapproved of free-thinking Arnold's substitution of literary culture for religion, Epstein comes out, finally and firmly, on Arnold's side: "He anticipated the issues of our day, and on every one his own position is admirable — admirable and tenable and usable in our time." Epstein deals largely with Arnold the literary critic, dismissing most of his poetry, such as "Dover Beach," as "anthology pieces." But is it so terrible to survive in anthologies?

But back, now, to 1880, the year of Geist's death, at the early age of four, and Arnold's elegy on his grave. Regretfully, we here give only a limited selection of the 20 — yes, 20 — quatrains:

Four years! — and didst thou stay above
The ground, which hides thee now, but four?
And all that life, and all that love,
Were crowded, Geist! into no more?

Only four years those winning ways,
Which make me for thy presence yearn,
Called us to pet thee or to praise,
Dear little friend, at every turn?

That liquid, melancholy eye,
From whose pathetic, soul-fed springs
Seemed surging the Virgilian cry,
The sense of tears in mortal things.

Stern law of every mortal lot!
Which man, proud man, finds hard to bear,
And builds himself I know not what
Of second life I know not where.

But thou, when struck thine hour to go,
On us, who stood despondent by,
A meek last glance of love didst throw,
And humbly lay thee down to die.

And so there rise these lines of verse
On lips that rarely form them now;
While to each other we rehearse:
Such ways, such arts, such looks hadst thou!

We stroke thy broad brown paws again,
We bid thee to thy vacant chair,
We greet thee by the window-pane,
We hear thy scuffle on the stair . . .

We lay thee, close within our reach,
Here, where the grass is smooth and warm,
Between the holly and the beech,
Where oft we watched thy couchant form.

Then some, who through this garden pass,
When we too, like thyself, are clay,
Shall see thy grave upon the grass,
And stop before the stone, and say:

People who lived here long ago
Did by this stone, it seems, intend
To name for future times to know
The dachs-hound Geist, their little friend.

Might a modern vet have saved young Geist's life? Possibly; but then he would not be likely to know the reference to the "Virgilian cry" in verse three above: [*Sunt hic etiam sua praemia laudi;*] *Sunt lacrimae rerum et mentem mortalis tangunt*, which is, of course, from the *Aeneid* — "[Even here, virtue hath her rewards] and mortality her tears: even here the woes of man touch the heart of man."

As to Arnold's point that he had written little verse lately: his last collection had been published in 1867. The Geist poem appeared in book form in 1885; it consisted of "elegies to a dachshund, a canary, and a liberal dean of Westminster."

GORM — German shepherd, a gift from the Queen of Sweden to Dr Axel Munthe (1857—1949); second-to-last of his many dogs.

Munthe was a Swedish doctor, writer-by-accident of a best seller, fanatic in his attachment to animals. He was physician to the Swedish royal family, and to the poor of the island of Capri. Munthe worked and studied with some of the greatest names in medicine — Charcot, Pasteur, Krafft-Ebing.

Munthe has been described variously as realist, mystic, scientist, poet, caustic philosopher, kindly essayist, and unsentimental fighter for animal rights. George Bernard Shaw called him "spokesman for man's conscience" — this, after a speech for the British Royal Society for the Protection of Birds.

Dogs, monkeys, bears, tortoises, a mongoose, an owl, a baboon, these were essential to Munthe's life, although he dealt in celebrities and royalty. This entry might also have been listed as under Lisa, Waldmann, Wolf, Barbarossa, Tappio, Puck — the names of other Munthe dogs (see below). His position on people who don't care for dogs: "There is nothing to do about such people but to pity them."

This trait may have been genetic. Munthe's older sister, a painter, after being widowed twice, filled her life with animals — dogs, cats, and parrots in the house; in the freezing Swedish winter "she carefully arranged reserves of food for tame mice and shivering rats."

Munthe received his medical degree in 1880, aged 22 — the youngest doctor ever admitted to the French Faculty of Medicine. He travelled to Italy and Sicily, where his escapades among thieves with his dog Puck, a German shepherd (or police dog, or Alsatian, as the breed is variously known) and companion at the time, later became literary material.

He also visited Egypt, and years later, in 1923, was one of the five scientists present for the legendary unsealing of the coffin of Tutankhamen at Luxor (*see* Abuwitiyuw). These five alone beheld "the royal youth in all his original beauty and magnificence, before the body crumbled away under their gaze."

At 24, Munthe suddenly married a very beautiful 19-year-old;

the marriage lasted eight years. Munthe, no dedicated family man, cut short his honeymoon and dashed off to work during the typhus epidemic in Capri, working non-stop in hovels and caves among the sick and dying. The islanders never forgot; the King of Italy awarded him a decoration, the first of many, which he "lost so often and never could find when friends wanted to see them."

Soon after, an earthquake struck Ischia in the Bay of Naples; and again, he worked there nearly single-handed. Three years later he again dashed off to work during the cholera epidemic in Naples, later describing the horrible scenes, the lack of equipment and personnel.

During the 1880s Munthe began publishing articles in Swedish journals — about mountaineering, about politics. They were always signed P.M., for Puck Munthe, the dog. Puck climbed the Matterhorn with his master, and Munthe had much to say on the subject of bravery — and foolishness. A heated correspondence from mountaineers followed; the dog always signed the replies "Puck Munthe, Member of the Alpine Club."

In 1907 Munthe married again, this time a beautiful young Englishwoman, and settled her in England. Two sons were born, but Munthe continued to be regarded as a bachelor, and made an "unconventional" husband and father. "I've known him all my life, and he just couldn't be married!" a London hostess once exclaimed to Munthe's son, saying that he must be "a six-foot mirage." The son loved his father, and analysed him well: yes, he was married, but he was "lonely all his life." As a father, he was "a friend beyond compare."

Just before WWI broke out, Munthe became a British citizen; Henry James was his sponsor. He served at the front and in 1916 wrote a violently anti-German book, *Red Star and Iron Cross*, which was banned in Germany.

Munthe's autobiographical fantasy, *The Story of San Michele*, published quietly in 1929, became to his astonishment a runaway best seller — 75 printings, millions of readers, and many translations. A biography, published after Munthe's death by his son and a friend (a Swedish baroness), is surely one of the few books of this genre whose index includes four dogs. His own book and his autobiography are interwoven with stories about animals, and they too list the dogs, and Billy the Baboon and other animals, in the index, an unusual boon to the dog researcher.

Munthe enchanted generations of readers in many countries, but there were also those who considered him a *poseur*, a name-dropper, busy manufacturing an image of himself as St Francis of Assisi. In this connection, *see also* "Ohren," the flea-bitten hound of Albert Schweitzer, who also became the object of criticism, charged with manipulating his "charisma" in order to work more effectively for his overriding concern, the "reverence for life." Interestingly, their two lives share many elements — both were doctors, both had their own deeply original views of Christianity, both lived far from the limelight, yet attracted celebrities to their rural abodes. Both were excellent musicians — Munthe on the piano, Schweitzer on the organ — and played beautifully purely for their own enjoyment. Both lived to be over 90.

In one of several prefaces he wrote for the many editions of *San Michele*, Munthe dealt with the question of accuracy of his memoirs, of whether he had "deceived" his readers:

In one respect at least I can say with a clear conscience that I have not deceived my readers — in my love for animals. I have loved them and suffered with them my whole life. I have loved them far more than I have ever loved my fellow man. All that is best in me I have given to them, and I mean to stand by them to the last and share their fate, whatever it may be.

If it is true that there is to be no haven of rest for them when their sufferings here are at an end, I, for one, am not going to bargain for any heaven for myself. I shall go without fear where they go, and by the side of my brothers and sisters from forests and fields, from skies and seas, lie down to merciful extinction.

Now about Gorm, the German shepherd given to Munthe by the Queen of Sweden when he was practising in Rome, before he left the field of rich patients and their often imaginary diseases. Gorm came from a German kennel and was still a puppy. When he arrived, Munthe was busy treating the Queen in her sick-room. The puppy ran away.

Her Majesty alerted the police, who searched for three days. No trace; and Rome was teeming with dog thieves. Then "something like a miracle occurred." Munthe happened to be walking past a shrub in the park in the Villa Borghese when he heard a faint whimper. He looked inside the shrub and found Gorm "crouched inside, half-starved."

This last-minute rescue from starvation made Gorm decide never again to lose track of his master. He was made watchdog of Materita (on Capri, where Munthe later lived), a post he stuck to all his life — until his master, in return for years of devoted service, shot him to spare him the pain of an infirm old age.

No sentimentalist, Munthe believed that old, infirm dogs should not be left to suffer, and he believed that shooting was the best, most painless way.

He also believed that it was essential to use dogs in experiments to discover a cure for rabies, then under investigation by Pasteur, in whose laboratory Munthe worked. And he was fearless. The peasants of Capri for years retold the incident of the doctor and the rabid dog that had been attacking workers in the field. It always escaped, and at night took refuge in the cellar of a deserted house, where no one dared to follow. Panic spread through the village, and the famous doctor was called. As soon as he heard the story,

he took out his revolver and loaded it. It was getting dark but two men had lanterns, and the three of them climbed the hill to the sinister ruin, from which issued periodic, long-drawn-out howls . . .

The Doctor entered the cellar alone, carefully feeling his way along the walls. Hardly had his eyes got used to the darkness when the dog sprang at him from a corner, foaming at the mouth. The next moment it collapsed, mortally wounded.

Idyllic daily walks on Capri with Gorm and Lisa, a miniature dachshund, were at the other extreme of experience. Gorm always

Dr Axel Munthe as a young man.

arrived for the walk at the Doctor's first whistle, while Lisa, like most dachshunds, had a mind of her own. Munthe was always very tolerant of Lisa and allowed her

to run about as she liked, for as he expressed it, she seemed to have so many affairs of her own to settle and always to have some fresh schemes in her head . . . usually concerned with catching mice (what would Schweitzer have said?). Yet whenever she chose to appear above ground, ears aflutter, Munthe always had something nice to say to her.

The Doctor finally found Lisa a mate with an equally elegant pedigree, at the Royal Palace in Rome. On Christmas Day Lisa "produced five replicas of herself, each the size and colour of a breakfast roll."

She was not Munthe's first dachshund. That honour goes to Waldmann, whom the then young doctor found while sightseeing at the castle of Heidelberg. (Actually, he was on his way by train from Paris to Sweden, in his capacity of accompanying a corpse, a

wonderful story, told in *San Michele*.) At the German castle, Munthe recalled decades later,

A dachshund puppy came rushing up to me as fast as his crooked little legs could carry his long, slender body, and started licking me all over the face. His cunning eyes had discovered my secret at first glance. My secret was that I had always been longing to possess just such a little Waldmann as these facinating dogs are called in their native country.

Hard up though I was, I bought Waldmann at once for 50 marks and we returned in triumph to the Hotel Victoria, Waldmann trotting at my heels without a leash, quite certain that his master was I and nobody else.

There was a charge at the hotel for a mess on the carpet, and at the station restaurant Munthe, informed that dogs were "*verboten*," put five marks in the waiter's hand and Waldmann under the table, and . . . But this marvellous story is really about a confusion of corpses, which few are likely to have read in the last 50 years. Highly recommended.

Should we find fault with Munthe for taking in only pedigreed dogs when the streets of European cities were filled with homeless, unhappy mongrels? Just possibly — but who are we to criticize a man who, because he could not endure seeing the cruelties suffered by trained animals in circuses, took one of the bears out for a day in the country? They travelled by train, Munthe paying both the circus and the railroad to provide one day's grace for that poor bear.

One of his most famous projects, in the early Thirties, was a campaign to end the lucrative business of catching small birds in nets on Capri; these were then sent alive to be served to the gourmets of Paris:

The birds! The birds! How much happier my life would have been (on Capri) if I had not loved them as I do! . . . Every spring it was a joy to hear them sing in my garden. But there came a time when I almost wished that they had not come. All they asked for was to rest for a while after their long flight across the Mediterranean . . . wood-pigeons, thrushes, turtledoves, quails, orioles, skylarks, nightingales, warblers, red-breasts, and many other tiny artists on their way to give spring concerts to the silent forests in the North.

A couple of hours later, they fluttered helpless in the nets; the cunning of man had stretched all over the island . . . In the evening, they were packed by the hundreds in small wooden boxes, without food and water, and dispatched by steamers to Marseilles, to be eaten with delight in the smart restaurants of Paris.

And how were the birds attracted to the nets? Munthe, trained in neurology, explains about the caged decoy birds used to attract the birds overhead by a constantly repeated call:

They cannot stop, they go on calling out night and day till they die. Long before science knew anything about the localization of the various nerve-centres in the human brain, the devil had revealed to his disciple Man his ghastly discovery that by stinging out the eyes of a bird with a red-hot needle, the bird would sing automatically. It is an old story, already known to the Greeks and the Romans . . .

In his campaign to end this traffic, Munthe approached the government in Rome, the Pope, and eventually Il Duce, Mussolini himself — the only man in Italy who backed him. Mussolini had been enchanted by *The Story of San Michele* and wanted to meet the author; they did, secretly, in Rome, and nobody heard a word about it. Soon after, Il Duce declared all of Capri a Bird Sanctuary.

But his victory cost Munthe dearly. ("The Latin races are notoriously cruel to animals," as his biographer put it.) Villagers poisoned two of his dogs — no better way of causing pain to their enemy — although he was also their doctor and saviour in medical matters.

The story of the butcher who profited most by the bird-netting is fascinating. Munthe twice offered to pay a large sum to buy the hillside of the nettings and was twice refused. Then the butcher became fatally ill and was given up for lost. Local diagnoses included pneumonia, stroke, evil-eye. Munthe was asked to come, and this time *he* refused.

I said I had never been a doctor in Capri except for the poor, and that the resident physicians were quite capable of coping.

Only on one condition would I come, that the man would swear on the crucifix that if he pulled through, he would never again sting out the eyes of a bird, and that he would sell me the mountain at his exorbitant price of a month ago. The man refused. In the night he was given the Last Sacraments.

At daybreak, his messenger appeared again. My offer had been accepted, he had sworn on the crucifix. Two hours later I tapped a pint of pus from his left pleura, to the consternation of the local doctor and to the glory of the village saint, for contrary to my expectations, the man recovered. *Miraculo! Miraculo!*

Munthe did not have much respect for the medical profession:

I had luck, amazing, almost uncanny luck with everything I laid my hands on, with every patient I saw. I was not a good doctor, my studies had been too rapid, my hospital training too short, but there is not the slightest doubt that I was a successful doctor.

He was far more sure of his excellence in treating sick animals, including the most dangerous at the Paris zoo. "Why could I put my hand between the bars of the black panther's cage and, if nobody came near to irritate him, make the big cat roll over on his back, purring amiably at me, with my hand between his paws?"

Why was he, and only he, able to lance the foot of a lioness who had been walking restlessly for a week on three legs? "The local anaesthetic was a failure, and poor Leonie moaned like a child when I pressed the pus out of her paw," but accepted the treatment with understanding.

HARRIS — Queen Elizabeth II's favourite Welsh corgi. Half-brother of Susan, favourite corgi of the Queen Mother, who has five others. Harris is of course also related to Apollo, Princess Anne's corgi. This ancient Welsh breed has long been associated with the British Royal Family, although there are some exceptions.

Harris is an important character in a marvellous book, *The Queen and I*, by Sue Townsend, about the Royal Family. First published in 1992 and reprinted many times, this is a sort of "socio-political science fiction" set in the very near future, about what would happen to the Queen and her family if the monarchy were abolished.

Comparisons with Virginia Woolf's *Flush* (q.v.) leap out at the dog-centred literary critic. Corgi Harris, unlike Cocker Flush, is not the main character, but he certainly appears in full, starting in the very first paragraph, in which Queen Elizabeth is in bed, with Harris, watching television. Harris yawns, "displaying his sharp teeth and liver-coloured tongue."

Stroking Harris's back, the Queen asks, "Are you bored with the election, my darling?"

Not a bad life, at old Buckingham Palace; the Queen buys "Good Boy" chocolate drops at Harrod's for her corgis. And then the election changes everything. No more Royal Family; but unlike earlier dynastic changes the Queen, her elderly mother, and all the others are not killed but are merely sent off to live in a poverty-stricken neighbourhood, with very few of their priceless belongings. And only Harris, of all the corgis, comes along. The formerly regal, formerly stupendously wealthy family now have practically no money, only bureaucratic procedures and state charity. The author appears to be a confirmed Socialist, but one with an incredible sense of humour, and with compassion for those at both ends of the economic rainbow.

The Queen comes out very well in her overnight descent from top to bottom. Prince Philip comes out badly — he lies in bed, refuses to eat. Princess Margaret is also an unpleasant personality. Princess Anne is great — practical, helpful, and ready to take on a boyfriend who is an illiterate carpet-fitter (he wins her heart by giving her a horse, Gilbert). Prince Charles is sweet, if hardly intellectually consistent, while Princess Di is a piece of foolish fluff. Their children quickly come to enjoy speaking horrible street English and running with the underprivileged neighbourhood kids.

Harris, too, quickly comes to like his new world:

He had started to hang round with a rough crowd. A pack of disreputable-looking mongrels, belonging to nobody in particular, it seemed, had started to gather in the Queen's front garden. Harris did nothing to discourage them; indeed, he seemed to positively welcome their marauding presence.

Then he begins running wildly through the streets with "The Pack," which include Kylie, "the pack bitch." Harris finds her exciting, though she could have used some grooming. Harris contemplates the fact that he had never been allowed to breed with anyone of *his* choice before: "all his previous liaisons had been arranged by the Queen." And then, in the middle of these rebellious, post–pedigree thoughts, Harris suddenly sees Susan, running along with the Queen Mother and a dear new friend, an immigrant woman from Jamaica. Harris never liked Susan, considered her a snob, and was jealous of her fancy wardrobe, on this day a "poncy tartan coat." Seizing the chance to upgrade his status with the Pack, Harris rushes to Susan and *bites her on the nose.*

Then Harris, congratulated by the Pack, goes with them to eat garbage from a fish-and-chips shop, and finally returns home covered with mud, smelling of fish.

Royal Family, dogs in simpler times. Little girl, left, is now Queen.

"You're nothing but a stinking hooligan, Harris!" says the Queen, and promptly gives Harris a bath with the last of her expensive lotion.

And so it goes — plenty of basic change and adventures for all the family, and a gorgeous interlude with a rather half-witted social worker who tries to explain to the Queen how to look positively on her new life. Until the very last page, when the Queen wakes up.

Again, Harris takes the spotlight: he is jumping up and down, barking ferociously at the TV. The Queen shouts at him to be quiet. David Dimbleby is "wearily" repeating that the Conservatives had won the election. It was all a dream; a nightmare.

In real life, at least in the gossip magazines, it is reported that the Queen's corgis hate the Queen Mother's corgis because the latter have royally luxurious pillows to sleep on.

HELENA — Last dachshund and close companion of William Randolph Hearst (1863 – 1951), American newspaper publisher, perhaps the most powerful who ever was. Helena was one of several Hearst dachshunds; framed photos of two others were in his bedroom. To one of them we might give the name "Rosebud," the psychologically-key-sled name in Orson Welles' *Citizen Kane*. This film, based on the life of Hearst, is the story of "an egomaniac power-mad acquisitive publisher and his drunken blonde ex-actress mistress living in a hilltop castle." As a result of this now classic film, Welles' name was banned from all Hearst publications.

Oblivious to all this (probably), Helena the dachshund lived happily and well at San Simeon, Hearst's spectacular castle in California. Today it is a tourist attraction, but far from what it was in the golden days of the Thirties. Much of the vast estate and its contents were sold when the Hearst empire began to crumble in the late Thirties.

Hearst loved animals and kept exotic species that roamed at liberty on his enormous estate; signs along the long approach to the castle read "Animals have right of way." But Helena was his favourite; and as will be seen, she was the only living creature that shared all-powerful Hearst's last hours.

Hearst's best-loved human companion was Marion Davies, the beautiful starlet 35 years his junior, who became his mistress until his death, and who presided over the incredible social life at San Simeon. In 1926 Hearst also built for Marion a "beach house" — it was compared to Buckingham Palace — at Santa Monica, where she could entertain her film friends. It was also intended to compete with the nearby "beach houses" of such as Douglas Fairbanks, Will Rogers, L. B. Mayer, and especially Marion's great rival, Norma Shearer. Marion's "beach house" had bathrooms and lockers for over 2,000 guest swimmers: "not very cosy," as one observant guest noted.

Hearst's wife, the mother of his five sons, lived elsewhere. The situation suited everyone (except, at heart, Marion, who very much wanted to marry Hearst). The five Hearst sons "were very fond of Marion, loved their mother, and adored and admired their father." A perfect arrangement — especially for one as big on Family Values as Hearst. It provides a larger-than-life lesson for the world that if you are sufficiently rich and powerful, you can have your "Family Value" cake and eat it too — even in those long-gone days of puritanical America, when "living in sin" was definitely a sin.

"No sexual intercourse between unmarried couples" was the most important of the three rules for guests at the Castle. Always excepting Hearst and Marion, who after a party would retire, via an elevator built for two, to their "Celestial Suite." Many of the ingenious guests managed to evade this cardinal rule, as well as the other two — "no drunkenness, no bad language or off-colour jokes."

At San Simeon, Rosebud was one of those dachshunds (and there was quite a collection of them among the rich and famous, as we are learning) who could sniff at some of the most famous legs in the world — Einstein and Churchill, movie stars Charlie Chaplin, Groucho Marx, Claudette Colbert, etc., etc. Parties might have a thousand or so guests, and nobody invited to the "ranch," as it was called, would dream of not accepting. Even the liberals, to whom Hearst was the arch-villain.

Here is Hearst to an editor who was publishing James Thurber's drawings:

Stop running those dogs on your page. I wouldn't have them peeing on my cheapest rug.

The great white father of "yellow journalism," who ruled his vast empire like a tyrant and revolutionized the way newspapers were run (though it is an open question whether some of today's sensational publications are any "worse" than Hearst at his worst), could not bear the thought of injury or death to any animal. Here is David Niven, often invited to the grand premises when he was a young actor, describing Hearst's concern for the littlest mouse. When the vast dining hall at the Castle became infested with them, Niven writes in his marvellous account, the

otherwise tyrannical Hearst,

far from destroying them, left out tasty titbits for them before retiring at night. When they multiplied alarmingly, he reluctantly agreed to have them trapped, provided they were not hurt.

Special cages were constructed to capture them alive, and each morning resentful Filipinos emptied the catch into the front garden. The little captives, hardly believing their good fortune, then hot-footed it happily back in the direction of the kitchen entrance.

Marion may have had a harder time than the mice, or Helena. Niven describes her as absolutely charming, and tells us that she and Hearst loved each other deeply. But she failed to become "Mrs Hearst," and like so many Hollywood personalities — each for his/her own reason — she became addicted to alcohol. And of course, that was forbidden; so all sorts of ruses were employed. Carole Lombard called that little beach cottage "Cirrhosis by the Sea."

Very interestingly, for our purposes, Hearst decided that Marion should play Elizabeth in the then hot property, *The Barretts of Wimpole Street* (*see* Flush). But the role had been set aside for her great rival Norma Shearer, who also happened to be the wife of Irving Thalberg, the designated producer. After long and bitter negotiations, Hearst ordered Marion's "bungalow" at

MGM to be towed across town to Warner Bros.

Hearst was born in California to a wealthy mine-owner and rancher. At 24 he decided to make it in journalism; he took no courses, but asked his father to buy him the small failing *San Francisco Examiner*. He built it up, bought more papers, and was soon a commanding power. He collected art, bought property, opposed America's entry in WWI, opposed the League of Nations, ran for Governor of New York. In his mid-seventies he still had amazing physical energy, and could hit an unreturnable tennis ball. He wanted to win.

But the last four declining years of his life were spent with Marion and Helena — in Beverly Hills; what was left of the "empire" was run by a boss-defying "committee." One of his last defiant acts was to buy 50 thoroughbred Arab horses and order them sent to San Simeon.

He died in August 1951, aged 88. Marion was at his bedside during his final night. At dawn the doctor gave her sedatives; when she awoke, Hearst was gone. The undertakers had obeyed earlier instructions from the "committee" to remove the body. The guards were also gone. A *Life* photographer took a picture of the big four-poster bed in which W.R. had died. Sitting on it, whining, was a little dachshund — his only companion when the end had come.

"HERMES" — Beautiful hound belonging to Alcibiades (c.450 – 404 B.C.), Athenian general and politician, described as "handsome, brilliant, charming, but absolutely unprincipled."

According to Plutarch, Alcibiades had a large and beautiful dog "whose principal ornament was his tail." Yet he had the dog's tail cut off "so that the Athenians should talk about this eccentricity rather than find something worse to say about him." And there was plenty of occasion for negative talk. An admirer and student of Socrates, Alcibiades "could not practise his master's virtues," and his behaviour strengthened the charges that "Socrates was corrupting Athenian youth."

During the Peloponnesian War, Alcibiades persuaded the Athenians to join an alliance against Sparta, "partly from policy and partly from private ambition." He was appointed leader; but just before the expedition, the statues of Hermes were "mysteriously mutilated." Alcibiades was accused of the crime, and also of "having profaned the Eleusinian mysteries."

We have bestowed Hermes' name on the dog because the images of both the pagan god — son of Zeus, often identified with Mercury — and the handsome dog were apparently cropped by the brilliant general. The god Hermes practically invited trimming, and not by merely a tail. His early cultist images were phallic; sometimes "a mere phallus served as his emblem."

Back to Alcibiades. After these accusations he was recalled from Sicily to stand trial, but escaped to Sparta. After many intrigues abroad and in Athens, he was finally dismissed and escaped to Phrygia, where he was murdered.

Not a nice man, and not nice to his dog, through whom we here recall him. He may even have brought about the fall of Athens. According to Thucydides, the Athenians — and "Hermes" too, with reason,

feared the extremes to which he carried his lawless self-indulgence, and . . . thought he was aiming at a tyranny . . . Therefore, though his talents as a military commander were unrivalled, they entrusted the administration of the war to others; and so they speedily shipwrecked the state.

HIM and HER — Beagles of President Lyndon Johnson (1908–73), 36th American President. Democrat, born and died in Texas. A work-addicted, controversial personality and master of Senate dealing, Vice-President Johnson succeeded to the presidency after the assassination of John F. Kennedy in November 1963.

Him and Her made the news in 1964 when Johnson, in an unfortunate photo-opportunity on the White House Lawn, was snapped grabbing Him's (or Her's?) ears and holding up the hound "to arouse yelps," as UPI reported, adding that the President claimed it "did them good." This naturally caused consternation among the nation's dog lovers. A spokesman for the American Kennel Club objected strongly, as did the Chicago Humane Society, which announced unequivocally that this was a very bad way to treat animals.

In this photo, several bankers stand in the background observing the ear scene. Two are laughing heartily (Republican machos?), two smile cautiously (politically uncommitted?), while one views the event with apparent disapproval.

Johnson was reported to have later told a staff member privately (if there is such a thing in the White House) that "he was going to lift those beagles by the ears until he trained them not to yelp."

As cruelty to animals goes, this is a very minor offense. But Johnson, facing his election as President that November, was supremely concerned with his "image" and with courting the press. Early in May, a few weeks after that unfortunate photo, he tried to make amends.

The "genuinely hospitable" idea was to invite all of Washington's journalists, with their wives and children — over a thousand in all — to a "party press conference," a "family frolic" on the South Lawn of the White House. Of course it didn't work, and was beautifully made fun of by the inimitable Russell Baker in the *New York Times*.

Amidst pink lemonade, data about corporate profits and Vietnam, kids crying "Mommy! Mommy!", sucking their fingers and grinding cookies into the lawn, as Baker reported, the grand finale came when the President let the kiddies mob him for a mass photo and "showed them the proper way to pet a beagle."

The beagle question had indeed come up earlier. Someone had asked, "Many of the young people here have dogs...Perhaps you would tell them the story of your beagles?"

The President's answer: "Well, the story of my beagles are (*sic*)

that they are very nice dogs, and I enjoy them, and I think they enjoy me, and I would like for the people to enjoy both of us." Following this less than magisterial reply, a much "meaner" question was asked — one, as Baker reports, about "over-exposure." The President "went into a slow burn."

Ah, how would FDR (*see* Fala) have handled the situation? Johnson, committed to liberal ideas, had a kind of fantasy that he was FDR's heir; but the Roosevelt style was from a planet other than his. President Roosevelt would not have dreamed of pulling Fala by the ears, even if he had been physically able. But then, Johnson's successor Nixon staged his Checkers (q.v.) media affair far more dubiously and infinitely less sincerely.

The realities that loomed behind Johnson's May-lemonade lawn affair were frightening. U.S. troops in Vietnam totalled over 15,000; U.S. planes were being sent to Laos; three civil rights workers were murdered in Mississippi. Krushchev was deposed in Russia; and the Chinese detonated an atom bomb. Dealing with problems was far more pressing than dealing with image-making. But Johnson on the campaign trail, stopping at small communities, perfected a winning style of "country oratory."

For all of their media exposure, the names of Him and Her never became part of American folklore, and their impact on Johnson's overwhelming November win over Republican Barry Goldwater has never been statistically estimated. After his election victory, Johnson said, on Christmas Eve, 1964:

I am going to build the kind of country that President Roosevelt hoped for, President Truman worked for, and President Kennedy died for.

It was, of course, not to be. Faced with the growing division in America on the Vietnam War which overshadowed all the other problems of his presidency, Johnson announced, in March 1968, that he would not run for a second term — the only American president ever to do so. The family and the beagles retired to the ranch at Johnson City, Texas.

JOFI — One of two chows loved, consciously and unrepressedly, by Sigmund Freud (1856 – 1939), Austrian psychiatrist, founder of psychoanalysis. The other beloved chow was named Lunyu. Besides the chows, Freud also lived on intimate terms with a German shepherd named Wolf. And so also, as we shall see, did his patients on the couch.

Freud's views on canines help to illuminate some of his views on the problems of men. In a letter to Marie Bonaparte, a fellow psychiatrist and fellow dog lover (she helped Freud when he was forced to leave Austria in 1938, when he was 82, by Nazi attacks on Jews), Freud briefly "analysed" his involvement with dogs:

They give us complete affection without duplicity; the direct simplicity of their lives is free of the inner contradictions of civilization that are so hard for us to deal with . . . (Theirs is) the beauty of experience complete within itself.

Freud did not hesitate to enter the usually forbidden territory of comparing canine characteristics with those of humans, and the latter came out badly in the Freudian view. In dogs he saw qualities that are lacking in mankind: dogs are honest and can be relied on. If a dog loves, he shows it. If he hates, he dares to show that too. Dogs, Freud wrote, are simply not capable of the "hypocrisy and deceit" of humans.

Freud even professed to admire "great beauty" in dogs when they were "hot-tempered." All in all, when contrasting their straightforwardness to the "pettiness" of "cultured" human beings, Freud gave the clear advantage to the dogs.

In his later years he always had one of his dogs present in his consulting room during analysis. Soon other analysts were following their master's lead and keeping *their* dogs in the room as their patients poured out their dreams, fantasies, and obsessions.

A Jerusalem psychotherapist who probably knew Freud years earlier used to do the same, and his dog was always under the couch during sessions. This Jerusalem dog's custom was to spring out suddenly from under the couch and, for no apparent reason, to begin to bark. If a new and startled patient would then glance at his watch, he would see that the hour was exactly up.

Born in Moravia, Freud was brought to Vienna with his family when he was four. He was interested in botany and chemistry, worked in physiological laboratories, and became a clinical neurologist, with a special interest in the then fashionable treatment of hysteria by hypnosis. In 1894, Freud made the revolutionary decision to replace hypnosis with "free association," and this became the kernel of psychoanalysis.

He soon attracted colleagues; some of them, notably Jung and Adler, then broke away and established their own schools of treatment. Long letters and discussions mark these ruptures: experts in the mysterious realm of the subconscious fight their battles just as inconsiderately as do ordinary people — as Freud so well knew when describing Jofi, Lunya, and Wolf.

Freud's theories and his names for the inner human landscape — the importance of sex from infancy; the formation and inter- pretation of dreams; the ego, superego, id and libido; the Oedipus complex, and all the rest — became very popular, especially in America, and not only among psychologists. Cocktail-party chat- ter was filled with references to "Freudian slips," wish-fulfilment, and let's-try-this-one dream interpretations. The 1963 movie *Freud* was a box-office failure, but did wonders for star Mont- gomery Clift.

Within the profession there were further breakaway move- ments: lay analysts, group therapy, behaviouristic and endless other offshoots, not to mention the post–Freudian pills for all problems. As has recently been noted, "the achievements of psychoanalysis held the seeds of their own undoing."

Volumes continue to be written evaluating Freud's revolu-

tionary contributions, from very pro to very con. "Trouble on the Couch" is a typical recent headline for a review of a multi-volume work entitled *The Rise and Fall of Psychoanalysis in the United States.* But as we now know, there was never trouble under the couch: there all was forthright and loyal and honest, with Jofi, Lunyu, and Wolf.

Freud's view of women is — currently — outdated. He expected them to be "gentle, adoring, compliant helpmates to men," and his patient, devoted wife "was not at home with his theories." But he took his family life seriously. He courted his wife long and patiently, and the couple had six children. One daughter, Anna, followed in father's footsteps and was not all that compliant. He must have been irritating at home, with comments like,

When a member of my family complains that he or she has bitten his tongue, bruised her finger, and so on, instead of the expected sympathy, I put the question, "Why did you do that?"

He was not a practising Jew and knew no Hebrew. In fact, he applied his psychological theories to religion (a "mass obsessional neurosis . . . patently infantile . . .") and considered it part of the world of primitive culture and mythology. In *Moses and Monotheism*, his last published work, written when he was over 80, Moses becomes an Egyptian, no less, who was killed by the Jews.

Understandably, this made Freud detested in many circles, with battalions of enemies left and right, Jewish and Gentile and atheist. The Vatican denounced psychoanalysis, while the Marxists, then in full swing, denounced Freud's "bourgeois decadent deceptions." Skeptical, pragmatic, self-deprived of the pleasures of religion and "idealism," pessimistic and often melancholy about the triumph of rationalism over superstition, Freud wrote, in an introduction to his published letters:

I do not think our successes can compare with those of Lourdes. There are so many more people who believe in the miracles of the Blessed Virgin than in the existence of the unconscious.

Dr Freud and the dogs, out from under the couch.

When Einstein wrote to Freud asking how, if at all, the curse of war could be abolished, Freud replied sadly that he had found no way to dispel the doubt that men will ever really be able to overcome their aggressions. Civilization, he wrote, is at best a temporary barrier, periodically breached by "all that is churning below."

For a closer look at the world of the chow and the Alsatian, we turn to another prominent Viennese behaviourist, nearly 50 years younger than Freud, who specialized in animals and wrote a raft of international best sellers — Konrad Lorenz.

Lorenz's footsteps must have crossed Freud's in Vienna, and their chows very possibly sniffed each other in a kindly, professional manner. Their owners' areas of interest overlapped — the nature of evil, of aggression, of behaviour modification, and much else.

Lorenz, like Freud a doctor of medicine, makes an important point for mothers who worry about dogs and germs. His own childhood was dogless, Lorenz writes regretfully,

> because my mother was born in a time when bacteria had just been discovered. Therefore well-born children tended to develop rickets because their milk was boiled to be totally sterilized, thus killing all the vitamins.

Because of this same fear of germs, he was not allowed to have a dog until he was able to swear, "on a man's word of honour that I would never let the dog lick my face." (*See* Pladumini.) Dr Lorenz's own children grew up from infancy, hale and hearty, in his "home zoo."

From physical to mental health: Lorenz's first dog, he recalls, was "unfortunately a complete idiot." It was a dachshund named Kroki (because he resembled a crocodile), who loved everyone indiscriminately — master, neighbours, thieves. Some dogs, like people, are just dumb, says our behaviourist, while some are simply "psychotic."

Freud and Lorenz differed in one crucial point: Lorenz was not Jewish, and in fact did nicely under the Nazis, with military service and academic appointments during WWII. One of his dogs was named Stasi — the same name as one of Hitler's Scottish terriers. Curiously, Leo Rosten, the very Jewish best-selling author on Yiddish and other subjects, named Lorenz (and also Freud) as one of his heroes, and that not too long after the war.

An even more remarkable chapter in Lorenz's rehabilitation was written by Victor Frankl, the Viennese psychiatrist who spent years in Auschwitz and other concentration camps. He then founded the "Third Viennese School of Psychotherapy (Logotherapy)," and wrote prolifically on behaviour, evil, and "Man's Search for Meaning." The point here is that around 1980 Frankl enjoyed a most agreeable discussion with Lorenz on the biological functions of behaviour. Lorenz "enthusiastically" agreed with Frankl, the latter reported with great satisfaction.

What stranger-than-fiction scenes the lives of Jofi and Lunyu can lead to! Chows, in any case, shared Lorenz's life — including chow–Alsatian mixtures. So, at least dogwise, he did not accept the principle of purity of breed. Pointedly, Lorenz wrote in his best-selling *Man Meets Dog* that breeding for looks and "championship" can create stupidity and nervousness. He would not dream of having a champion in the house, he made clear, because "overbreeding" has led to the downgrading of chows, of Scottish terriers, and worst of all, pugs (*see* Trump). All this was written by Lorenz 30 years ago: the situation is of course far worse today.

Nor did post-war Lorenz champion male superiority in dogs. He considered bitches more intelligent and loyal than male dogs, with a finer character, and far better as companions. "How strange that in English the term should have become so negative!"

While granting huge distinctions between individual representatives of all breeds — and of all mixtures — Lorenz gives top marks to chows for complete and deep understanding of the master. The breed was also marked by a certain "restraint" and — a good one for Freud — "for lack of sentimentality and excessive demonstrativeness."

He describes at length the mutual impact of dog-personality on owner-personality, and the choice of "parallel character" or "complementary character" for which we love our dogs. His wife's chows, Lorenz writes admiringly, were always clean and tidy, while his own were always wallowing in mud! No wonder *Man Meets Dog* was a runaway best seller in many languages 50 years ago.

In his post-war political correctness, Lorenz describes Thomas Mann's Bashan (q.v.) story as "the most beautiful depiction of the soul of a dog," pointing out that it is no coincidence that the dog was a mixed breed.

Without mentioning the master's name, he takes serious issue with the way Freud, like so many others, "compare" dog and man. Lorenz disliked the "bad and very wrong" notion that "animals are better than people." True, the fidelity of a dog has no counterpart in human social loyalties. But the dog (as Freud, too, indicated) knows nothing of the "labyrinth of often contradictory social relationships" in which mankind is caught. (Patriotism? Persecution?) Even the most loyal dog, Lorenz notes, is in human terms "amoral."

Lorenz's final chapter deals with mortality, with the death of a much-loved dog. His point is that when a dog dies, he can be replaced — although never with an identical creature. But it is good, for purposes of immortality, if the dog's descendants are still in the family.

Freud was distraught when Jofi died, and allegedly often hummed an aria from *Don Juan* in memory of their relationship. This was surely the chow's due; for no other dog — except of course Lunya and Wolf — contributed so much to the dawn of psychoanalysis by cheering up the Master. They were the very first in a long line of psychiatrists' dogs who, down there under the couch, heard the daily "retrieved" outpourings of broken romances, repressions, wish-fulfilment, slips of the tongue, in themselves immortalized in Freud's much translated and re-published 1914 best seller, *The Psychopathology of Everyday Life*.

A pity it contains no speculations on the meanings of all those twitches, mini-snarls, and repressed yips that we have all noticed as our dogs lie dreaming.

(opposite) Best-selling former showgirl Jacqueline Susann.

JOSEPHINE — Well-promoted, well-connected small black poodle, heroine of her own book written by her loving owner Jacqueline Susann, former showgirl and stupendously best-selling author of the Sixties and early Seventies.

Susann's *Valley of the Dolls* sold 356,000 copies in hard cover and another ten million in paperback. Not bad, and who cares that the novel was despised by the critics. Nor was it a matter of good luck. "Jackie" and her husband Irving Mansfield had put together the most carefully detailed, high-powered sales campaign in the history of publishing. The results proved the value of Public Relations, and of the financial, if not the lasting literary value of the book.

Jackie Susann's third book, *The Love Machine*, published in 1969, also became America's #1 Best Seller soon after publication, thanks to hugely publicized TV appearances, cross-country tours, etc. This second best seller had been preceded by a "moderate" success, *Not Tonight, Josephine*, about her beloved poodle, Josephine.

Not long after *The Love Machine*'s stupendous sales, poor Josephine the poodle died. Susann's husband telephoned the couple's devoted and dedicated publicity and PR person, Abby Hirsch, to see what might be done about Susann's bereavement.

"Abby," said the worried husband, "I don't know what's going to become of Jackie. She's taken to her bed. It's very bad."

Abby thought briefly about how she might console Susann, and then decided to try for an impressive obituary: a little publicity, expert Abby knew, cheers up anybody. And the poodle, after all, "was more famous than most people" and deserved some fitting memorial. The Duke and Duchess of Windsor, she knew, had

loved Josephine; in her prime she had been "adored" by Richard Nixon (*see* Checkers), and "had slept with Richard Burton."

Hard-working Abby spent hours on the phone trying for Josephine's obituary. She quoted (accurately or not) Nixon's comment on this poodle:

> Some dogs have heart and some dogs have brains. Josephine is the only dog I ever met who had both.

Nothing helped; the media would not accept the "dead dog story." Even though not long before, the dog element had been prime on TV prime-time, when Susann's *Love Machine* was being attacked by a critic. "I'd rather see dogs fornicate than read your love story," he shrieked at Susann on the David Frost Show.

In response, a man ran down the aisles and shouted at the critic: "I have read *Every Night, Josephine*, and I would rather see dogs fornicate than listen to you talk." The studio was in a frenzy, and it was all marvellous publicity.

Susann's spectacular best-seller successes were, it was widely agreed in the publishing industry, the result of tremendously hard work (with her husband and press agent Abby) in the kingdom of publicity. Jackie Susann, Abby wrote — in the present tense — in a book that appeared in 1974,

> is not simply a best-selling author. She is also, by design, a very visible author . . . She's in the public eye, attractive, successful, a "star" as well as an author.

Her last novel, *Dolores*, made less of a splash, even though it contained lines like, "He had wanted to go to bed with her, but she was expecting the hairdresser at eight in the morning." It may be that Susann, although still attractive and far from elderly, was no longer up to the rigours of sales promotion. For although very hard-working — and lucky — publicity can do wonders for instant sales and shooting stars, it can do nothing to assure the remembrance of books past. Nor can it assure long life for the author. By the time Abby's book appeared, Jackie Susann was dead, of cancer, in 1973.

LOBENGULA — Celebrated London bulldog who enjoyed life at the offices of the elite literary newspaper, *The Pall Mall Gazette*, edited by his master, Harry Cust, in the 1890s.

The London News Agency became interested in Lobengula when word got out among the top people about his arrival at the *Gazette*. In December 1893, the News Agency sent a letter to a Member of Parliament requesting more information on this matter. Such was the tone of (some) British journalism a century ago:

You mentioned last Saturday that the dog sold to Mr Cust was to be kept at the *Pall Mall* office and that there are already a number of dogs of various breeds quartered at that office ... (We are) interested in the matter and would be glad if you could jot down a few notes of what you saw at the *Pall Mall* office, that is, about the dogs, about Cust's personal appearance, whether he is a judge of dogs, etc.... Also, could you supply a photo of the pup's mother or father or both. If you could jot down these points tonight or tomorrow and send them along to the office, we shall be much obliged.

P.S. We particularly want a complete pedigree of the dog sold to Cust.

Contributors to this paper "written by gentlemen for gentlemen," and those who wrote letters to the editor in this golden corner of British journalism (yellow was also an emergent colour) orbited in a galaxy of talent as well as of dogs. Many had superb pedigrees in this Victorian *Who's Who* that included Oscar Wilde, Swinburne, H. G. Wells, Rudyard Kipling (*see* Vixen), and Wilfrid Scawen Blunt (whose wife was a grand-daughter of Byron, *see* Boatswain).

The job of editor had been given to Cust not long before —
across the dinner table, and accepted on the spot — by none other
than William Waldorf Astor, 1st Viscount, great-grandson of
John Jacob Astor and grandfather of . . . But enough. The idea is
clear — a happy gathering of elegant snobs.

Cust himself, as his nephew Sir Ronald Storrs makes passionately clear, was a "golden personality of dazzling promise";
everything that he did he did with "incomparable ease and grace."
But it has been said by a later, and unrelated historian, he was
"flawed by self-indulgence" with regard to women, to whom he
was "irresistibly fascinating," and so his public career never
fulfilled its early promise.

Cust edited *The Pall Mall Gazette* from 1892 to 1896 "as a
Conservative paper, and gave consistent support to the
Progressive cause." He died in 1917 at 56. Years before, he
wrote a sonnet commemorating Lobengula.

For the historical record: Lobengula was the name of an
African chief in South Africa, where Cecil Rhodes was bearing
Kipling's "White Man's Burden" in the profitable imperialist
conquest of diamonds and gold. In 1893, the year of the letter
about the bulldog's pedigree, far off at the British settlement of
Victoria in Africa, Lobengula's braves attacked the whites. He
was defeated in the "Matabele War," was driven from his capital,
Buluwayo, and became a fugitive.

LOBO — Katherine Hepburn and Spencer Tracy's mutt — "part police dog, part coyote, one ear up, one ear down, half the size of a police . . . Half his tail was gone."

Earlier in her long and remarkable screen career, Hepburn had dogs. She was once photographed with three of them — Peter, Button, and Mica, two blacks and a white, apparently spaniels, being gazed at with radiant fondness by the beautiful Hepburn.

But because Lobo was the dog she shared with Tracy, and because the nearly 30 years with him — in his house, but outside of marriage — were the most important of her life, this is the dog Hepburn describes. Lobo had

the warm humour of a mutt — bright — handsome head elegantly marked — big eyes full of joy. He was my friend and went everywhere with me. He had a snooty manner and his nose turned slightly up. Fun. Anyway, you can see I liked him a lot.

Probably not every mutt was allowed to enter the Beverly Hills Hotel tennis court. But this was famous star Hepburn and Lobo was her escort — Spencer Tracy was already very ill, and Hepburn left their "illicit" house for a while every day to play tennis.

It was during this difficult period that Lobo performed the very important role of bringing Hepburn together with Tracy's daughter Susan, whom she had never met. Susan's mother was Tracy's wife and their Catholic marriage persisted, theoretically and indissolubly, in the face of the widely known 30 years of "mortal sin." Hepburn had never met his grown children.

Lobo's scene went like this. Hepburn and the mutt went through the gate into the tennis court.

All of a sudden, almost following us, came a girl — blushing madly — the blush spreading over her face — up to her neck— but she was determined.

"It's Lobo, isn't it?"

"Yes," I said. "Yes, it's Lobo." Who — who? Could it be? Yes it is, I thought, Susie — it's Susie. Spence's daughter.

"He looks fine."

"Yes, he's fine, Susie."

Suddenly we were at a loss for words — silence.

Then I: "Look Susie, if you would like to get to know me, that can be very easily arranged. You know where I live and you know the telephone number. Any time . . . "

So she called. And we became friends. Just like that . . .

Just like that — because of Lobo. He was about three at the time, although called "Old Dog." He had arrived towards the end of the Tracy–Hepburn relationship, which had produced nine films. The last, *Guess Who's Coming to Dinner*, was completed not long before Tracy's death in June 1967.

Lobo and Hepburn were, as usual, alone with him that last night. Tracy, as usual, could not get to sleep; Hepburn, as usual, did all that she could, which amounted to dedicating her life to his comfort and wishes:

I said, well, go on, go to bed. And I'll lie on the floor and talk you to sleep. I'll just talk and talk and you'll be so bored, you're bound to drift off.

Well, I went in and got an old pillow and Lobo the dog. I lay there watching you and stroking Old Dog. I was talking about you . . . and about my studio and your new tweed coat and the garden and all the nice sleep-making topics . . .

The millions of readers who enjoyed Hepburn's best-selling autobiography encountered Lobo only towards the end of the book. They had been waiting eagerly for the Spencer Tracy part; Hepburn wisely kept them waiting, and when the time came, in the last chapters, Lobo, too, entered the story. The book, breathlessly written, is a compelling account of Hollywood scenes and of an enduring romance. Hepburn revered Tracy as an actor, and as a man. The complexities of living in sin as a "bad" Catholic were incomprehensible to her, who came from an unconventional upbringing — her mother had been a suffragette, her physician father supported her mother's causes.

LUCKY — President Ronald Reagan's big Bouvier des Flandres bitch. She was a gift to the 40th President of the United States soon after his inauguration in 1980, and apparently created none of the furore that had surrounded the acquisition of Checkers (q.v.) by his predecessor, President Richard Nixon. This may be attributed either to the easy-going atmosphere of the early Eighties (and to Reagan's sweeping victory over Democrat Jimmy Carter) or to Reagan's sunny disposition and personal popularity, which had hardly been Nixon's attributes.

The problem with Lucky was something quite different. The Bouvier des Flandres is a large Belgian dog that has been bred for herding instincts, and also for work with the police and the military, although its "working intelligence" is ranked at only 29. Its specialty is cattle, but available presidential couples will do, as happened in the case of the Reagans. Lucky, it soon became apparent, was constantly trying to

herd the President, nipping at his heels and even drawing blood on at least one occasion. She also jumped up on Mrs Reagan, in the sort of sideways bumping manner occasionally used by big herding dogs to nudge their charges so that they move in particular directions.

The "photo opportunities" provided by Lucky herding the President and First Lady became embarrassing. The Reagans loved her, but her specialty made her a poor White House attraction (for comparison, *see* Millie). She was therefore sent off to the Reagans' big ranch in California, where there "were animals to herd, rather than politicians."

As a matter of fact, one of the commands used by shepherds to control herding dogs is curiously, if unintentionally appropriate to the political world. It goes:

"Go left" or "Go right," as required. "The dog moves in the direction indicated, the movements being relative to the position of the flock." Or of the public — depending on the issue and the pressure of political forces.

LULU — Small Japanese dog, related to Pekingese, who shared
the bed and declining years of Ethiopian Emperor Haile Selassie
(1891 – 1975, deposed 1974).

A servant at the palace in Addis Ababa during the Emperor's
last years was interviewed by a visiting Polish writer. The servant
reported that Lulu (a male) slept on the Emperor's huge walnut
bed, in which the Emperor himself, by then old and frail, was
"lost among the sheets."

During official ceremonies, according to this more than eye-
witness account, Lulu often sat on the Emperor's lap, but had the
habit of descending "to pee on dignitaries' shoes."

The august gentlemen were not allowed to flinch or make the slightest
gesture when they felt their feet getting wet. I had to walk among the
dignitaries and wipe the urine from their shoes with a satin cloth. This
was my job for ten years.

Lulu's autocratic urination takes us back to a ruler who was
front-page news half a century ago. Haile Selassie I, who ruled
Ethiopia (Abyssinia — and earlier still, Sheba) from 1930 until
deposed by his son, had been known in his early days as
"progressive . . . and the focus of the aspirations of the younger
modern generation."

Going back much further in the complex history of this area,
we come to the Queen of Sheba, whose son, by King Solomon,
according to tradition founded the empire c.1000 B.C. And then
there was Judith, a Jewish princess who, about 960, "conceived
the design of murdering all the members of the royal family" and
ruling in their place. The infant heir was spirited away by loyal
adherents, while Judith reigned for 40 years.

Christianity was introduced in the 4th century, and the first
bishop of Ethiopia was consecrated around 330; Coptic Christianity has long been official. But the religious and political
history, both before and after, is a hopeless account of invasions,
influences, persecutions, quasi-kingdoms, missionaries (Protestant, Roman Catholic) and so on. As Gibbon put it, "encom-
passed by the enemies of their religion, the Ethiopians slept for

near a thousand years, forgetful of the world by whom they were forgotten."

Modern wars have also swirled through the area: the Italians arrived in 1870; the first Italian war followed. European influence increased, and "chaos reigned." Haile Selassie, then known as Ras Tafari, became regent in 1917 and ruled together with his aunt, Empress Zauditu, a "delicate arrangement."

Cutting short much slaughter and intrigue: in 1923, Haile Selassie outlawed slavery, making it punishable by death, and that same year he brought Ethiopia into the League of Nations. He assumed the title "Negus" (King) in 1928, and was crowned Emperor in St George's Cathedral in Addis Ababa ("new flower") in 1930, taking his new name, which in Amharic means "Might of the Trinity."

In his prime, the Emperor's exotic animal companions tended to be large felines, especially the lion — for he was, of course, the Lion of Judah. Little Lulu was for the end. But the choice was still appropriate. Lulu was most certainly an Inuko, a "Lion Dog" (*inu* is Japanese for dog). This is a very small breed closely related to the Chinese Pekingese, but with a black mane and face. It is known for its bravery and aggressiveness.

And then, as many still remember, the Italians invaded Ethiopia in 1936. The Emperor fled to Palestine, where he is still recalled walking the streets of Jerusalem's Old City in exotic gold-trimmed dress; and then on to London. British forces, together with Ethiopians, liberated Ethiopia in 1941 and the Emperor returned, "the first of the heads of state expelled by fascist conquerors, the first forced into exile, and the first to return."

All this is by way of introduction to our real concern, the Emperor's last days, with Lulu. By then, aged about 82, he was very frail. He weighed little more than a hundred pounds, ate less and less, slept very little, arose at three or four in the morning. "When he was alone he dragged his feet and swayed from side to side." But when he knew that someone was watching him (other than Lulu), he forced himself, with great dignity, to move so that "his imperial silhouette remained ramrod-straight."

This, his last year, was a period of civil war; a revolution broke out in February 1974. The aged Emperor began every day by listening to informers' reports. He did not trust the printed word.

In this surrealist sequence of scenes, the advantage of the spoken word was clear: "If necessary, the Emperor could say that a given dignitary had told him something quite different from what he had really said, and the latter could not defend himself with written proof."

But he never showed any sign of irritation, nervousness, anger, rage, or frustration . . . His nerves were cold and dead, like steel . . . His Highness knew how to develop and perfect this quality, on the principle that in politics, nervousness signifies a weakness.

And what was happening out on the streets? Chaos, intrigue, and violence during the period before the Crown Prince deposed his father in September 1974. The Emperor was placed under house arrest in his palace, where he died in August 1975, six months after the monarchy was abolished.

During those last months with Lulu, before the Emperor's arrest, everyone spied on everyone, everyone was searched for secret weapons. Sounds of gunfire. Dogs (the underprivileged ones) barking everywhere. Addis Ababa was

a dog city, full of pedigreed (*sic*) dogs running wild, vermin-eaten, with malaria and tangled hair.

As the Polish writer, present at the doomed royal palace, put it,

They caution me again, needlessly: no addresses, no names, don't say that he's tall, that he's short, that he's skinny, that his forehead is this or his hands that . . . Or that his knees — there's nobody left to get down on your knees for.

Once again the darkling plain of Matthew Arnold (*see* Geist) is humanity's movable scene, and not only in Africa, with the "confused alarms of struggle and flight / where ignorant armies clash by night."

LUMP — Dachshund of Pablo Picasso (1881 – 1973), prodigious Spanish painter, whose progress through various periods (post–Impressionism, "Blue," Cubism) has been termed "an encyclopaedia of 20th century art."

At various times during his long life, Picasso also kept Kabul (an Afghan hound), Jan (a boxer), and cats. But his animal collection is nothing compared to the women in his life; as has so often been said in one form or another, the importance of his mistresses and wives was "prominent if sporadic." In his paintings, women evolve in changing guises; but interestingly, Picasso chose animals to express his view on artistic progress:

> God is really only another artist. He invented the giraffe, the elephant and the cat. He has no real style. He just goes on trying other things.

Dachshund Lump appears in an apocryphal tale, one among the many about his owner. In this one, the Master painted a rabbit on a piece of board, and Lump attacked and ate it, thus enabling the teller of this one to add that he was "the only one ever to eat an original Picasso." In another apocryphal anecdote — surely pre- or post–Lump — the artist was asked what he would save if his studio caught fire. His answer: "My cat."

Picasso was born in Málaga, the son of a teacher of painting. His good friend Gertrude Stein (*see* Basket) said of him, "The character, the vision of Picasso is like himself, it is Spanish." And in a fine Stein–Picasso mix, she went on that

> he does not see reality as all the world sees it, so that he alone among the painters did not have the problems of expressing the truths that all the world can see, but the truths that he alone can see, and that is not the world the world recognizes as the world.

In 1904 he moved to France, having begun to create legends about his past. At 25, in 1906, he had already produced 200 paintings and hundreds of drawings. He attracted the attention of an important dealer, Vollard, who later said, "Each new picture by Picasso is met by the public with indignation, and then their amazement changes into admiration."

As the world knows, he became a public figure — a millionaire artist (in many media, including sculpture and no less than 2,000 pieces of ceramics) and a violent anti-fascist during the Spanish Civil War: his *Guernica*, painted in 1937 after the Germans bombed the Basque town, was seen in Paris and New York.

After the liberation of Paris he made headlines by joining the Communist Party, an act that has been described as less ideological than sentimental. The millionaire painter, it has been suggested, was unable to compensate for his artistic independence and loneliness by love for one woman; perhaps the Party, he said, might give him a "family." So somehow even Lump, Kabul and Jan, not to mention his various legitimate and illegitimate children, failed to satisfy Picasso's needs; for "family," he joined the party that had called his works "bourgeois decadent."

Picasso was so self-centred that his human relationships were tragedies. One of his mistresses, Françoise Gilot, wrote of his "Bluebeard complex" that made him "want to cut off the heads of all the women he had collected in his little private museum." Describing Picasso's constant referrals to her predecessors, Gilot wrote that she began "to have the feeling that if I looked into a closet, I would find a half-dozen ex-wives hanging by their necks."

The painter himself, on women:

For me there are only two kinds of women — goddesses and doormats.

And:

Every time I change wives I should burn the last one. That way I'd be rid of them. They wouldn't be around now to complicate my existence. Maybe that would bring back my youth, too. You kill the woman and you wipe out the past she represents.

Between the ages of 85 and 90 he produced more than 400 drawings and engravings. Paris celebrated his 90th birthday by showing eight Picassos in the Louvre in the place of Leonardo's *Mona Lisa*.

LYCAS — Simonides' hunting hound. The first great Greek lyric poet, Simonides of Ceos (c.556 − c.468 B.C.) wrote dirges, odes, hymns, and epigrams, of which only fragments still exist; among a great many other works was his epitaph on the Three Hundred at Thermopylae. He won 56 poetry competitions, was enormously popular, and did very well financially. Simonides was accused of avarice by later writers, from Aristophanes onwards, because his poems "could command any price."

According to Plutarch, he also wrote the following epitaph for his beloved hunting "bitch," Lycas:

> *Although beneath this grave-mound thy white bones now are lying,*
> *Surely, my huntress Lycas, the wild things dread thee still,*
> *The memory of thy worth tall Pelion keeps undying,*
> *And the looming peak of Ossa, and Cithaeron's lonely hill.*

Extravagant praise? Possibly; but we may be sure that this was written in genuine love and sorrow since Lycas was in no way a source of money to the poet.

Simonides and Lycas lived well. Most of the poet's long life was spent at the court of various patrons of literature, first at his native Ceos, then at Athens, and finally at Sicily. Simonides was so celebrated, and so In with the right people, that he was on occasion even a political force and was able to bring about a reconciliation between two enemies.

How did he find time to go hunting with Lycas? He was a scholar as well as a poet, and according to tradition, introduced the distinction between long and short vowels, and adopted the Ionic alphabet. "Mnemonics," the system or art of improving memory has been credited to Simonides, but it was probably developed later and Simonides received the credit because of his phenomenal memory into old age.

MAF — Poodle given by Frank Sinatra to Marilyn Monroe (1926 – 62), movie star and sex symbol, whose short and tragic life and death have raised many questions and much speculation.

Maf's full name was shortened by Marilyn from the original one, which was no less than Mafia — a little joke, obviously, because of Sinatra's alleged connections with the "Family" (*see* "Mafia").

Marilyn's full name was originally Norma Jean Mortensen, and then Baker through her first marriage. At the time of Maf's arrival, she was married to intellectual playwright Arthur Miller. The union, which astonished the gossip world and was not expected to last, did not.

Marilyn's much publicized relationship with President John Kennedy (several dogs, a horse, a cat, rabbit, and hamster) also gave rise to much speculation — as, of course, did the young President's assassination.

The "Blonde Bombshell," as the press enjoyed calling her, had little luck with men; and like other women who radiated sex on the stage and screen (*see* Delores), she must have felt surest of the love of her dogs and other animals. Besides Maf, Marilyn lived at various times with mongrel Cindy, basset hound Hugo, collie Muggsie, and cats Mitsou and Persian.

This is, in any event, an intensely canine network of speculations: Frank Sinatra's dogs included Labrador Leroy Brown and Miss Wiggles, the spaniel.

"MAFIA" — Miniature pinscher accustomed to snuggling in the satin-gowned lap of high-living murderer Salvatore Lucania, aka Charley "Lucky" Luciano (1897–1961). "Family boss" of organized crime in New York in the Twenties and Thirties. Succeeded to the title of "Public Enemy #1" in New York, where he had a suite at the Barbizon Plaza Hotel, after the death of Al Capone.

Lucky's lucky little dog is here called "Mafia" (origin of name unknown; unknown, too, is the name of the photographer who took this photograph in 1955 [?], immortalizing Lucky and Mafia on some quiet evening at home back in Italy, after release from jail in America).

Capone, familiarly known as "Scarface," had built up an empire in Chicago based on bootleg beer, extending to slot machines, laundries, and unions. It grossed about $60 million a year, back when the dollar was the dollar. To guard his empire Capone had his own "army" of about a thousand men, all inherited by Lucky. "Scarface" miraculously survived his rivals until finally convicted of income tax invasion.

Lucky's pampered pinscher, part of an unusual "Family," could as easily have been called Cosa Nostra (Our Thing), a more recent name by which the hard core of organized crime became known in the U.S. The complicated code of traditions of the Mafia — hierarchy of power, intermarriage among members, and much gore — already existed in Italy in the last century, and probably came to America around 1860. For the record, Cosa Nostra was thought to have about 5,000 members in 1970, in a nationwide federation of 24 groups known as "Families." It controlled most of the gambling, loansharking, extortion, narcotics, hijacking, securities thefts, and other rackets. Would you want your miniature pinscher to have puppies with a Cosa Nostra pinscher?

The Mafia had also been called the Syndicate, the Mob, Organization, Black Hand, the *Unione Sicilione*. With so many shifts in organizational name, the name of one little dog is a small matter; so are specifics about its sex, and eventual fate.

Lucky Luciano, holding his beloved dog, appears to radiate
kindness. Could such a man harm even a flea on Mafia's tail?
Born in Palermo, Sicily, heartland of the Mafia, the boy was

brought to America when he was nine. He was arrested for the first time the next year for shoplifting (aka "pinching" — a clue to his love of pinschers?). Luciano rose in the Mafia ranks and reached his peak during the great underworld war of 1930 − 31, which began in New York and reached Chicago, where Al Capone was coming to the end of his reign. During a period of 18 months, there were 50 murders within the Mafia, none of which were ever solved. One of the top generals, "Joe the Boss" Masseria, was killed by the treachery of our Lucky, who was one of his lieutenants. According to a Mafia informant, the rival general was shot to death in his Park Avenue office because he was trying to kill off *his* rivals, including Luciano. But Luciano and his underboss hit first, hiring two members of a Jewish gang to kill the General early in 1932. (To avoid even more confusion, we are not filling in all the top Italian names, but their gang names are illuminating: "Mad Dog," "The Shadow," and later "Three-Finger" and "Joe Bananas.")

With the well-planned death of the second general, Lucky Luciano became Family Boss. He ruled until 1936, when an ambitious young prosecutor named Thomas E. Dewey (who had a cat) got him convicted of compulsory prostitution. The sentence was up to 50 years in prison. Lucky's associate in the helpful hit managed to flee to Italy, where he became a favourite of Mussolini.

Not Lucky. In jail during WWII, in a cell presumably well-padded with extras, he helped the Allies re-create the Mafia that Mussolini had tried to destroy: opposition to fascism was strongest in Sicily, and in Piedmont in the north. This became part of a Mafia legend, on the grounds that its earliest origins contained certain "chivalrous" elements.

So Lucky was pardoned in 1946 and deported to Italy. He died in Naples of a heart attack in 1961. After a gala funeral in Palermo, his body was returned to the U.S. for burial. Much of the family was there — perhaps including his Neapolitan mistress, Igea Lissari (whose dog appeared to be a Scottish terrier).

A Mafia will probably always be with us. The accents change: Russian and Latin American are now in style.

MATH — Favourite greyhound of King Richard II of England (1377 – 99). According to just one source — Jean Froissart, 14th century French chronicler and thus a contemporary of Richard's, who spent most of his life in royal courts — Math deserted his master at the castle of Flint when it became clear that Richard was about to be deposed. According to this scoop of Froissart's, which appears in none of the other many sources describing Richard's tragic career, the greyhound then shifted his loyalty to Richard's enemy (and former friend) Henry of Lancaster, known as Bolingbroke.

This is the only known case of disloyalty among dogs of famous owners. Can it be attributed to Richard's very problematical personality? Probably not, even though this king, who died in prison at the age of 22, has been described as "the most enigmatic of the kings of England . . . one of the many unfitted to rule, hated and unsuccessful."

In any case, is this enough to put off a dog from his prevailing trait of loyalty? Perhaps a post–modern dog psychiatrist might suggest that Math was simply trying to maintain his own mental health in the face of Richard's own constantly shifting allegiances and policies. (For views of dogs afflicted by their masters' neuroses, *see* Nero, Boatswain.)

But perhaps the problem of the disloyal dog story may be found elsewhere: in Froissart himself. (This theory is purely that of the editor.) For this raconteur and historian (1338? – 1410?) lived in the era of courtly love — passion as prescribed by strict convention and unwavering fidelity. His view of loyalty, and his taking the dog to represent the worst of all sins, may perhaps be explained by the tale of his own sad passion:

One day, near a castle in France when he was not yet 18, working as a clerk and "like all clerks" absorbed by the idea of love, he saw a "demoiselle" reading a book of romances. He wrote down all the details — the title of her book, "the singular beauty of her blue eyes and fair hair."

But the demoiselle scornfully refused to speak to him; she even "seized him by the hair and pulled out a handful." She never changed her mind. Perhaps, it has been suggested, Froissart then undertook his life of wanderings and the writing of voluminous chronicles, which cover the period 1325 to 1400 — a time of battles and murderous conflicts. He was wherever things were happening, and he met everyone who was anyone and wrote it all down, in what has been called "literature" rather than history. Among many other important figures, he met the young Richard before he became King, and his "Chronicle" ends with the murder (if that is what it was) of Richard II.

Shakespeare does not use "Math" in his play, and as noted, Froissart is the single source. However, just to set up a mood of scholarship, the reader is invited to consider a few of the footnotes to Shakespeare's *Richard II* in the scholarly Arden edition. We must start with some that deal with the question of Which Horse was ridden by Bolingbroke, both at his coronation and on rides into London. (But we will get from the steed to the greyhound.)

At the very end of the play, just before his murder, Shakespeare has Richard ask his former groom about Bolingbroke's horse. The groom answers that it was Richard's own roan, Barbary, "That horse that thou so often hast bestrid / That horse that I so carefully have dress'd!"

Richard miserably remembers how he ate "bread from my royal hand . . . Would he not stumble? Would he not fall down / Since pride must have a fall . . . "

Richard then apologizes to the horse for blaming him for mankind's ways. With respect to these lines, the footnotes suggest that perhaps Shakespeare made up the whole incident; but on the other hand, we are told, some sources suggest other possibilities . . . and finally! Yet another scholar suggests that Shakespeare may have derived the incident from Froissart's story (vi.369) of how a greyhound of Richard's

left the fallen king to fawn upon Bolingbroke in the court of Flint Castle.

But, we are then told, "this does not seem very plausible." So perhaps, after all this, canine loyalty does remain unblemished.

MILLIE — World-famous, media-wise springer spaniel brought by Mrs George Bush to the centre of Washington political life in 1987; to the White House as First Dog in 1989.

Millie's Book, a *New York Times* best seller published in 1990, is one of those literary works "allegedly" written by the animal, with some devoted human assistance (in this case, First Lady Barbara Bush herself, plus additional human assistance). The book is short, bright, easily readable, and actually an album of "photo opportunities" with VIP's for which Millie was a marvellous focal point.

Even uncompromising Democrats, provided they love dogs, could only have been enchanted by the sight of President Bush caught forever kissing Millie's nose on their very first date, before George and Barbara and Millie went on board Air Force II. Or seeing George, now President, on the White House lawn playing with Millie and her puppies. Or noting that Millie took for granted lying on the white presidential rug at the Prez's feet in the Oval Office with a yellow tennis ball in her mouth, while he mused on matters of state.

Carping scholars might complain that Millie in fact missed a great opportunity in failing to extend her material and writing the definitive work on a hitherto neglected subject, Presidential Dogs. (An excellent, sadly neglected potential device for sneaking aspects of American history into the minds of reluctant students.)

For example, Millie provides not a word about Fala (q.v.). He was, to be sure, a Democratic and not a Republican dog, but the Bushes and the Roosevelts might at least have enjoyed some bi-party canine conversations. And one finds not a word about Checkers (q.v.), who was thoroughly Republican, but possibly an embarrassing type of spaniel.

If only in passing, Millie does mention her predecessor at the Vice-Presidential House, one C. Fred Bush, who belonged to Barbara's husband. But not a word about his temperament, or even his breed. President Coolidge's dog appears (*see* Rob Roy), but only because of the painting. What an opportunity was missed, considering the access to the archives!

Millie does, in fact, come across as just a trifle self-centred. In this overly psychological era, this may be because she was traumatised by Barbara Bush's now famous first words to her when they met:

You are so sweet, but you are so ugly. You have a pig's nose, you are bow-legged, and your eyes are yellow.

Millie then notes that she knew she would "have to try harder," but that Barbara also said that she really loved her. And that after this "rocky start" Barbara was soon telling others that Millie was the best dog ever, and that "she will never have a male dog again." A correct, if belated discovery, because female dogs are certainly the finest companions.

Considering Millie's exalted surroundings and exceptionally loving family — three generations of them — it is perhaps no wonder that she was a bit stuffy about her pedigree and her pure bloodline, and was terribly hurt when referred to as a "mutt" in the Washington press. Millie should be the first to realize that a pedigree is not everything, that many pure-bred dogs, especially in our day, are stupid and sickly; and that the world is full of eager "mutts" who would give their souls for a small part of Millie's world. Mutts who would not dream of eating the White House garden tulips, as Millie so blithely did, and reported with such unconcern.

(The term "mutt," by the way, is American slang originating c.1910, an abbreviation of "mutton-headed"; it meant "ignorant blunderer," and by way of contempt, a small dog. It may be doubted that Millie ever looked that up. Did she ever look up the source of that over-used word "pedigree"? It comes from the French *pie [pied] de grue*, or crane's foot, so called from a 3-line mark used in denoting succession in pedigrees.)

Such post-literate quibbles aside, it is not in the least surprising that this book delighted so many readers. It was a refreshing change from the disasters of human politics, while making the First Family marvellously human before our very eyes. And it must surely be every dog's dream to appear on the cover of *Life*

Magazine, as Millie did in May 1989: to meet kings and queens, heads of state and movie stars and statesmen and sportsmen; to fly here and there by private plane; and to loll about on and under the elegant beds and settees of America's most famous house.

Barbara Bush wisely and generously donated all proceeds from sales of the book to her Foundation for Family Literacy. And at the same time and with relative ease, she turned Millie into the most famous dog that ever lived, anywhere! And did so almost instantly, as things are done today.

There are two runner-ups behind Millie — Nipper (q.v.) and "Tobi" (q.v.), neither of whom have ever had nearly the status to put them, say, on T-shirts. Nipper was once seen by millions, but few could know his name or his story. As for "Tobi," the apocryphal dog whose name came only later, how many people across two millennia of relatively limited literacy have read the *Book of Tobit*? One can only hope that more widespread literacy will retain its four-syllable value.

We so appreciated your warm welcome to Millie's puppies. All are doing well and we send our best wishes.

Barbara Bush   George Bush

MONSIEUR GRAT — Pampered dog of René Descartes (1596 – 1650), French scientist and philosopher; founder of the school of philosophy called "Cartesian." A mathematical genius, Descartes invented analytical geometry. His influence on the development of science and philosophy was enormous, although some of his principles were later upset by Isaac Newton.

Relying exclusively on reason, Descartes adopted a "quasi-mechanical conception of the universe" — and of the human body as well. As a devout Catholic, he believed that human beings possessed an immortal soul, while animals did not: they were "simply machines with no consciousness and no intelligence." No dog could ever say *"Cogito, ergo sum"* (neither, today, could most college graduates).

But as psychologist Stanley Coren has pointed out in his intensive survey of canine capabilities, Descartes himself had a pet dog at home called "Monsieur Grat," and the great denyer of dogs' capacity for emotional responses talked to Monsieur Grat just as besotted owners have done through history. "He worried about the dog's health and referred to things that the dog liked or did not like, and sometimes privately speculated on what the dog might be thinking."

On the problem of immortality and whether dogs have souls, we can do worse than to quote James Thurber (1894 – 1961), who dealt with psychology via cartoons and humour:

If I have any beliefs about immortality, it is that certain dogs I have known will go to heaven, and very, very few persons.

In the case of Catholic Descartes, the contradiction between the private and public lives of scientists need not concern us here. We note merely that "a certain Hélène" bore him a daughter, who died young. Descartes lived in Holland for 21 years and was a friend of the family of Prince Rupert, and possibly also of Boy (q.v.). He died at the Swedish Royal Court, where he had been invited by Queen Christina, and where he found the weather too cold. (Italy had been too hot.)

MUSIC — Favourite greyhound of poet William Wordsworth (1770 – 1850), chief of England's "Lake Poets." Once known for his revolt against the artificial poetry prevailing during his youth, Wordsworth later became wordy and less interesting. And after an early round of enthusiasm for the French Revolution, he turned politically conservative with age and prosperity — the usual process. Appointed Poet Laureate in 1843.

Music and three other of the poet's dogs — Dart, Prince and Swallow — are the subject of a later Wordsworth poem, "Incident Characteristic of a Favourite Dog." It is basically a tragedy, and a tribute to Music's character.

The writer was living in rural England, which he always loved. What happened: one morning the Master goes on his rounds through the pastures, checking the cows and sheep. His companions are four dogs, "each pair of different breed / Distinguished two for scent, and two for speed." Music and Dart, the speedy ones, are greyhounds; the other two, breed unspecified, must also be hounds.

All four dogs start chasing a hare, who knows just what to do: run for the river, "crusted thinly by a one night's frost." The hare makes it safely across, to the poet's relief. All the dogs follow, but oh! The ice breaks, and Dart, Music's greyhound partner, is deep in the river.

> *Better fate have Prince and Swallow —*
> *See them cleaving to the sport!*
> *Music has no heart to follow,*
> *Little Music, she stops short.*

She is a loving creature, the poem continues, and what she tries to do is save her friend Dart struggling in the water:

> *From the brink her paws she stretches,*
> *Very hands as you would say!*
> *And afflicting moans she fetches*
> *As he breaks the ice away.*
> *For herself she has no fears,*
> *Him alone she sees and hears,*

Makes efforts with complainings; nor gives o'er
Until her fellow sinks, to reappear no more.

Where was the Master — the all-observant poet — at this fatal moment? Did he jump into the icy water to save Dart? The poem would surely have recorded such heroism.

When Music died, much later and at home of old age, Wordsworth wrote another poem as a tribute to this much-loved family dog. He explains why he set no stone monument over her grave — this is what men do for men; for the dog, only the big Oak will mark the grave. In this, Wordsworth was unusual, and unlike many other famous owners (*see* Boy, Lycas, and many others).

Music's last days, carefully described by Wordsworth so long ago, were just like those that afflict modern, vet-treated old dogs. The human family hoped the end would come soon,

For thou hadst lived till everything that cheers
In thee had yielded to the weight of years;
Extreme old age had wasted thee away,
And left thee but a glimmering of the day . . .

Poor old Music was deaf and very feeble, and although death was a welcome release, the Wordsworth family all cried when it came. Music had shared so many "household thoughts," and she was, as so many owners have claimed through the ages, a somehow special dog, with "precious boons vouchsafed —

Found scarcely anywhere in like degree!
For love, that comes wherever life and sense
Are given by God, in thee was most intense;
A chain of heart, a feeling of the mind,
A tender sympathy which thee did bind
Not only to us Men, but to thy Kind . . .

Wordsworth's voluminous writings include many poems about nature — birds, flowers, lambs. A few quotations still linger — "The world is too much with us . . ."; "Our birth is but a sleep and a forgetting . . ." Poetry is "emotion recollected in tranquillity."

William Wordsworth.

And of the enthusiasm of the early days of the French Revolution:

> *Bliss was it in that dawn to be alive*
> *But to be young was very heaven.*

But as classics go, Wordsworth is gone, and widely unread

today. Who today can recall "The White Doe of Rylstone," a tragedy in which the surviving daughter of a family of Catholic rebels in the time of the Scots revolt (*see* Mary Stuart's "Bonny") is comforted by visits from a white doe?

A little gossip may help to modernize Wordsworth. In 1791, during a visit to France when the revolutionary spirit was still for liberty and before the Terror, he was profoundly impressed by it all. He also fell in love with Annette, daughter of a French surgeon. A baby, Caroline, was born. Wordsworth abandoned Annette (like Dart, in the icy water?) and returned to England, torn by remorse both personally and for mistaking the French cause. He made his home in the Lake District with his sister Dorothy, and later married a childhood friend, Mary.

Another strange aspect of Wordsworth's career was his friendship and long literary working relationship with Samuel Coleridge, whose nature and character (and addiction to opium) could not have been more different. Yet the two collaborated on a book of poems, living in close contact until the break came several years later. Poor Coleridge stumbled into the house of their mutual friend Charles Lamb (whose dog, Dash, appears in Lamb's letters) mumbling "Wordsworth, Wordsworth has given me up!" (Dart again?)

Wordsworth's arrangements, especially his marriage, were not easy for his sister Dorothy, on whom he so depended. She was a talented writer herself, and it is thought that both her brother and Coleridge were in the habit of taking "good lines" from her notebooks for their work.

His final acceptance by the Establishment and appointment as Poet Laureate gave Browning (*see* Flush) a subject for attack:

> *Just for a handful of silver he left us,*
> *Just for a riband to stick in his coat —*
> *Shakespeare was of us, Milton was for us . . .*
> *He alone sinks to the rear and the slaves.*

As for the lasting value of the "Music" poems — well, probably none but the dog lover would now be interested. How would the

story be presented today? Best as a TV cartoon, in which sentimentality may still thrive.

Here is yet another Wordsworth poem about canine fidelity:
"Fidelity." Again, it begins with a shepherd on his rounds. He
suddenly hears and then sees a dog. But it is not "of mountain
breed," and it is very shy. There is something unusual in the dog's
behaviour. Nobody is around.

The shepherd follows the dog through difficult, isolated,
precipitous country, and suddenly discovers a human skeleton
on the ground. The shepherd then remembers that a traveller had
passed by three months earlier. The dog had guarded the spot,
and his dead master. This, Shepherd Wordsworth thinks, is a
wonder, and deserves "a lasting monument of words":

> *The Dog, which still was hovering nigh,*
> *Repeating the same timid cry,*
> *This Dog had been through three months' space*
> *A dweller in that savage place . . .*
>
> *How nourished here through such long time*
> *He knows, Who gave that love sublime;*
> *And gave that strength of feeling, great*
> *Above all human estimate!*

Finally, in memory of Music and her master, excerpts from a
still contemporary quotation on an always relevant theme — our
being "out of tune" with nature:

> *The world is too much with us; late and soon,*
> *Getting and spending, we lay waste our powers:*
> *Little we see in Nature that is ours;*
> *We have given our hearts away, a sordid boon! . . .*
>
> *Great God! I'd rather be*
> *A pagan suckled in a creed outworn;*
> *So might I, standing on this pleasant lea,*
> *Have glimpses that might make me less forlorn;*
> *Have sight of Proteus rising from the sea;*
> *Or hear old Triton blow his wreathed horn.*

"NELL" (left) **and "GWYNNE"** — (names undoubtedly incorrect), a huge hound and a tiny King Charles spaniel, very well behaved, posing — or else painted in later — with five children of Charles I of England and Ireland (b.1600, beheaded 1649).

This beautiful portrait by Van Dyck was painted several years after the Flemish artist had been knighted by Charles I and appointed court painter. The boy is the future Charles II, born 1630 and therefore about ten years old at the time. His sisters? One of them might be Mary, born 1631, who married William of Orange. Two other girls were born later; three children died in infancy.

"Nell" and "Gwynne"? The names here attributed are purely mnemonic devices. For Charles II, seen here as a good-as-gold, thoughtful little boy, grew up to be a cheerful, personally-pleasant king, "immoral" but "interested in science." He has also been described as "unscrupulous, corrupt, selfish, but more successful" than his father, Charles I, who had this painting done, and who faced his execution bravely. (His private life was "without blemish" — no Nells, as in his son's last thoughts.)

Charles II had no legitimate children but a whole series of illegitimate ones by his many mistresses, of whom the most famous was the witty actress Nell Gwyn. On his deathbed 50 years after this serene painting was made, his last words were said to have been "Don't let poor Nelly starve."

The era of both father and son — uncle and cousin of Prince Rupert (*see* Boy) — was marked by almost incessant warfare, by complicated religious conflicts between Catholics and Protestants, by political warfare between Royalists and Parliamentarians and between Scotland and England. Only readers with a super-sound education in English history can keep all this straight. As a 50-year-old encyclopaedia sums up Charles II, "closer study is modifying many of the older verdicts" of "notorious lasciviousness."

He himself once said that he "was no atheist, but could not think God would make a man miserable only for taking a little pleasure."

NERO — White mongrel terrier, third member of the family of Thomas Carlyle (1795 – 1881), renowned Scottish writer, and his wife Jane Welsh Carlyle (1801 – 66), who would have been a famous writer if she had lived a century later.

This particular husband-terrier-wife triangle was ultimately tragic for all, as Virginia Woolf points out in *Flush* (q.v.). Nero was Jane's dog, and he apparently gave Jane the constant love her husband could not. When Nero died after being hit by a carriage, the event so upset Jane, who had supposedly recovered from a serious illness, that she died soon after.

Carlyle, once greatly renowned for his essays and histories, was the son of a poor stonemason. He met Jane Welsh, daughter of a wealthy doctor, when she was a precocious and witty girl. She had written a tragedy when she was 14, and was engaged to marry her tutor. She broke the engagement and married Carlyle in 1826. Early in their relationship, the two planned to collaborate on a modern version of Abelard and Heloise, a project never completed.

One of Carlyle's most important works was his massive biography of Frederick the Great (*see* Alcmene), whom he greatly admired. A lively controversy after Carlyle's death suggested that he also shared some of Frederick's other traits: one of his many biographers believed that "Carlyle was one of those persons who ought never to have married." Everyone knew that he was sickly, melancholy and unstable, although he lived to be 86.

Whatever qualities Carlyle may have shared with Frederick, enthusiasm for dogs was not one of them. He often found Nero irritating (or was it just jealousy?) and once tossed the dog out of a top floor window. It was retrieved by the cook, and recovered.

Jane needed everything Nero could give her, although the Carlyle home was a centre for literary VIP's. After her death in 1866, Carlyle discovered from her diary how much she had suffered from his temper and "want of consideration."

She has been described as one of the finest letter-writers in the English language. Like many gifted women of her time and earlier, the literary talent was revealed only in her letters and diary. The couple's frequent temporary separations were difficult, Nero, of course, remaining with Jane, but so were their times together. When they were apart, Jane wrote Thomas a letter every day, and expected him to do the same.

But what would this brilliant, cranky, insomniac, infirm, opinionated husband have made of some of the letters Jane sent him, purporting to come from that annoying dog? Here, for instance, is what she wrote to her husband on Tuesday, January 29, 1850, from their house in Chelsea. It is signed "Obedient little dog, Nero":

Dear Master,
I take the liberty to write to you myself (my mistress being unable to write to you she says) that you may know Columbine (the cat) and I are quite well, and play about as usual. There was no dinner yesterday to speak of . . .

Jane goes on in Nero's voice to tell Carlyle all sorts of things he surely has no interest in hearing, such as about the dog and cat's supper. At this period, Carlyle was "attacking the shams and corruption of modern society"; his *Oliver Cromwell* had been published, and he was preparing for Frederick and Voltaire. He believed strongly that "History is Biography," while cute little Nero continued in his own vein, Jane serving as secretary:

This is a fine day for a run; and I hope I may be taken to see Mohe and Dumm. They are both nice well-bred dogs, and always so glad to see me; and the parrot is great fun when I spring at her; and Mrs Lindsay has always such a lot of bones, and doesn't mind Mohe and Dumm and me eating them on the carpet. I like Mrs Lindsay very much.

We will not even consider any possible reply to Nero from Carlyle, already known as a "man who hated everybody and everything," and who, when asked the population of England, answered, "Thirty million, mostly fools."

In a vain attempt to win the heart of the master, who a few years later would throw the dog out of the window, the Nero — Jane letters go on:

I left off last night, dear master, to be washed. This morning I have seen a note from you which says you will come tomorrow. Columbine and I are extremely happy to hear it; for then there will be some dinner to come and go on. Being to see you so soon, no more at present from your

Obedient little dog,
Nero.

If Jane was trying to grasp for attention for herself, and for her relationship with her dog, she expressed this problem clearly in a letter to a friend (not to her husband). "I too am here!" she wrote a decade after her marriage:

In spite of the honestest efforts to annihilate my I-ity, but merge it in what the world doubtless considers my better half, I still find myself a self-subsisting and alas! self-seeking *me*.

She goes on to quote a child in a story by Goethe, who "speaks out with the charming truthfulness of a child" — or a dog, as the Carlyles had instead — what Jane is "perpetually feeling, although too sophisticated to pull people's skirts, or exclaim in so many words, 'I too am here.'" Yet she had chosen her domineering husband for "a warm true heart to love me, a towering intellect to command me, and a spirit of fire to be the guiding star, light of my life."

After Jane's death, which followed so closely the death of Nero, Carlyle fell into a deep depression. By his 80th birthday, the Sage of Chelsea was a national fixture, and congratulations poured in, including one from Bismarck (*see* Tyras). He had continued to write, but according to critics, his later works have less value than the earlier ones, when he still had "domestic problems."

NIPPER — Smooth haired fox terrier, trademark on emblem of *His Master's Voice* on phonograph records. Much more famous than his master Marc Baraud. Until the invention of cassettes and alternative entertainment such as TV, Nipper was second in fame and immediate recognition, if not by name, only to Presidential spaniel Millie (q.v.).

Nipper was a real dog who lived in a real home with his beloved master. Barraud's family had come to England from Paris more than two centuries earlier as refugees, Huguenots persecuted by the Catholics. There were many painters in the family — Marc's father, who specialized in painting animals; his uncle; and his brother Francis, who had a successful atelier in London.

By the close of the century Marc was retired and living happily with Nipper. He loved puttering about with carpentry, and had recently bought that marvellous much-discussed invention, the gramophone. (*See* Tyras.) The top pop song of the day was a waltz, "After the Ball," sung by Irish tenor Dan Donovan. Little Nipper loved the song and could hear it over and over again; in fact, he loved his master's new record-playing device almost as much as he loved to eat.

An account of Nipper's rise to stardom — which begins with a tragedy — has come down to us in some detail. In this story, one fateful evening Nipper ran over to Marc, sat at his feet, and snuffled at him expectantly.

"Yes, yes, Nipper," said Marc. "Just be patient, in a moment you'll get your little concert." Marc had been fussing about with his new gramophone for so long that Nipper was impatient. Marc carefully carried the phonograph — a rather ugly contraption on a box with a big black rubber funnel — into the salon, made the necessary preparations, and with trembling fingers placed the needle on the line of the waltz. Then Marc sank into his armchair.

The scratchy tones of "After the Ball" emerged from the funnel. As always, Nipper sat transfixed before the apparatus, ears up, intent and motionless as a statue. The song came to an end, the sign of the record's conclusion began to rotate over and over again. Nipper happily went to his master and gazed up at him thankfully. But this time there was no reaction from Marc. He was dead in the armchair.

After his brother's death, Francis took over his possessions, including the gramophone and Nipper. He had an easy time with the former; it did exactly what it was told. Not so Nipper. He missed his departed master so intensely that he would never obey orders, never came when called, behaved badly, and even refused to eat. He would not budge from the gramophone apparatus. Nipper did not really belong to his late master's brother, but to the phonograph, which he seemed to view as the symbol of his real "master's voice."

Francis was patient, understood the situation, and was impressed by Nipper's loyalty. Often, while at work painting portraits in his atelier, he would turn on the phonograph just as a favour to Nipper. The dog would sit motionless in front of it, listening intently with his dark brown ears, and day after day the strains of "After the Waltz" would fill the room.

One day Francis had an inspiration. He put a new canvas on his easel and began to paint the dog and the phonograph. "I wish all my subjects would sit so perfectly still and well-behaved for their portraits," he muttered to himself. When the painting was finished, he gave it the title, *His Master's Voice.*

Francis's painter friends did not think much of this work. The dog, they said, looked fine; but why the apparatus with its ugly black funnel? Nevertheless, Francis took the painting to the offices of the Edison and Bell Phonograph Company and showed it to one of the representatives, asking if they might be interested in the painting.

"Ah . . . we like the phonograph," the Edison man said politely. "But why is the dog in the picture? But leave it for a few days. Perhaps we'll get used to the dear little animal."

Francis agreed and returned home, where he found one of his painter friends waiting for him. He'd been thinking it over, said the friend, "and I think it's that damn black funnel that bothers me. There should be a bright, gleaming brass funnel. Then you might be able to sell it. More gleam, more gold!"

Furthermore, the friend continued, a new little gramophone company had recently opened in Maiden Lane and there, without doubt, Francis could find the appropriate brass funnel. Francis hurried to the new company's offices and explained his predicament: he needed a brass phonograph funnel in order to paint a particular dog in a particular scene.

The Managing Director of this little firm was an American, William Barry Owen, who realized the value of brand identification in the best American sense; this scene occurred in the spring of 1899, but America was already far ahead in the world of corporate competition.

Owen thoughtfully examined the painting after Francis had retrieved it from the other less far-sighted company. He suggested alterations, and ordered 12 copies of the picture. Thus was born one of the most famous trademarks of all time.

Nipper himself died a few years later, and was buried in the little garden behind Barraud's studio. Barraud himself died in 1924. That same year, the "Gramophone Group" spent close to ten million pounds sterling to publicize Nipper. He was by then immortal, the best-known dog in the world, staring endlessly at that old-fashioned phonograph on millions upon millions of records all over the world.

"OHREN" — German for "ears"; name given here to brown-and-white mongrel dog of Albert Schweitzer (1874–1965) — doctor of theology, doctor of philosophy, doctor of medicine, musician, humanitarian, Nobel Prize winner for Peace in 1952.

Born in Alsace, Schweitzer spoke only German and French, and he did not really call this dog "Ohren" — it seems to have had no name at all. It has been bestowed here because the most noticeable thing about this dog were his permanently bandaged ears (see below). He was one of Schweitzer's countless and constant, loving and beloved animal companions at the leper colony hospital in Lambarene, Equatorial Africa, which Schweitzer directed for over 50 years.

Why were Ohren's ears permanently bandaged? Because Schweitzer was known not only for his love of animals but also for his reverence for life, and this took extreme forms. Thus he did not permit the removal of the ticks that infested his constant companion, whose ears were therefore always sore — but neatly bandaged. Schweitzer also opposed swatting mosquitoes. Screening was permitted, but he preceded later environmental concerns by decades: insecticides were strictly forbidden, as were vehicles (except for jeeps), electricity, and most modern "frills."

During his long lifetime, Schweitzer wrote about 200,000 letters, all by hand, at night, by an oil lamp. A baby antelope was usually asleep under his old wooden desk, which he had made himself; his devoted jackdaw would be sitting on his shoulder.

Many names other than "Ohren" could have been bestowed on this nameless mutt, or on any of the other unpedigreed canines that were always part of the Lambarene family. We could have called him "Kant," because Schweitzer wrote his theological thesis on Kant's philosophy of religion in 1899 (and later wrote a psychiatric analysis of Jesus). We could have called him "Bach": the doctor's monograph on Bach was published with a critical edition of Bach's organ works, and he continued playing Bach on a decrepit organ every night in the jungle. And the dog certainly could have been named "Rev" — short for reverence for life, the underlying precept at Lambarene.

Asked about the criticism so often levelled against him, that he showed more concern and far more affection for animals than for humans, Schweitzer would reply, "True. Because humans can take care of themselves." Yet his professional life at Lambarene was devoted to helping the poorest of the poor, and the most abandoned of the Africans — the lepers.

In the course of time he attracted a constant stream of visitors, including the rich and famous, to his not easily-accessible hospital. He also became the target of criticism, and opinions were divided as to his motivations: some were sure he was a saint, others that he was creating his own myth (essential for raising money to support the hospital). In all this, there is a certain similarity to the story of Dr Axel Munthe (*see* Gorm).

Many fascinated guests have described the paradoxes of life at Lambarene. Dinner, for instance, was served at a long wooden table set with beautiful German china and cutlery brought long ago from Schweitzer's native Alsace to the jungle. The doctor presided at the centre of the table, with Ohren always next to him.

Many witnesses confirmed the recurring story of what happened whenever a group of visitors walked with Schweitzer along a jungle trail and happened to cross the path of a colony of ants. "*Achtung!*" the doctor would call out, and then everybody had to take great care not to step on an ant.

He was hale and hearty for his 90th birthday party in the jungle in January 1965; Ohren, it may be assumed, was no longer of this world but had been supplanted by another mutt. Schweitzer died later that year, after 52 years in a leper colony far from sanitation and "progress," surrounded by grieving lepers, friends, and animals.

PELLEAS — Bulldog puppy of Maurice Maeterlinck (1862–1949), Belgian dramatist, poet, writer on philosophy and nature; Nobel Prize winner for literature (1911). The short, happy life of Pelleas, who died at seven months, is described in warm detail and with much speculation about fate in Maeterlinck's essay "Death of a Young Dog."

The author, described as a "neo-Romantic symbolist," was greeted in 1890 as "a new Shakespeare" when his drama *The Princess Maleine* was produced in Paris. He also wrote children's books that were classics for years: *Maya the Bee* and *The Blue Bird of Happiness*. Widely translated were his *Intelligence of Plants*, *Life of Termites*, and *Life of Ants*.

Pelleas the puppy was born in Paris and given, complete with name, to Maeterlinck, who brought him to his estate in Belgium. The name was probably meant "ironically," Maeterlinck notes: his drama *Pelleas and Melisande*, written in 1892, at least lives on in Debussy's opera.

"Why should I have renamed him? Will the name of a human, or of an imaginary hero, be in any way diminished when bestowed on a poor, lovable, loyal, honourable dog?"

Pelleas the puppy did not live long enough to meet his Melisande. "In his short existence, he had no past. His clever eyes opened only long enough to observe the world and to love mankind, and then closed again before the secret injustice of death." Maeterlinck avoids sentimentality — and plot — in his little memorial to the bulldog. Instead, he manages to achieve his aim of "indicating the mystery which lies just out of sight, beneath the surface of ordinary life . . . with a symbolism so realistic as to be almost bare."

By contrast, the human Pelleas in Maeterlinck's drama that attracted Debussy suffers plenty of plot: he loves his brother's wife Melisande, and is killed by him. But she was merely "playing" at love and dies in childbirth, "guilty but also innocent."

Briefly happy, bulldog Pelleas, with his "mighty forehead arched like that of Socrates or Verlaine, his little black pug nose pushed up into an unsatisfied affirmation..." must learn so much in so little time. Maeterlinck points out that a puppy has to grasp rapidly the rules of conduct and of existence "in a world he never made." Human children have years in which to learn what is allowed and what is not; a puppy, in just a few weeks, must learn how to behave in the bedroom, the study, the kitchen ("that place with the marvellous smells"); about earth and sky and water and snow, about where and how long one sleeps, about how to behave towards his brother dogs, towards chickens and geese . . . And then the dangers of the street . . .

Yet throughout, his supreme joy comes from "feeling on him the hand of the God to whom he has given himself."

The dog is utterly different from all other living creatures, because only the dog is totally bonded to man. As a result (at least, neo-romantically symbolically!) the dog is infinitely luckier than all the rest. He alone

occupies a truly privileged place, a unique and enviable position. He is the only living creature that has found and acknowledged an undeniable, palpable, unduplicable, ultimate god . . . He has no need to seek out from the dark any complete, higher, infinite power for the absolution of lies, hypotheses, and dreams.

He has a morality higher than anything he can discover within himself, and which he can exercise without thought or fear. He possesses the complete truth, a positive, incontrovertible ideal.

Maeterlinck assures us that his puppy, until he died of what appears to have been distemper, was in fact totally happy in a way that we can never be. "He would lie by my desk, tail carefully tucked under his feet, head a bit to one side the better to observe me, at once quiet and alert, like a saint in the presence of God."

PERITAS — Hound of Alexander III, known as The Great (356–323 B.C.), King of Macedon, conqueror of most of the civilized world of his day. According to Plutarch, Alexander loved this dog, almost certainly a hound, and named a town after him. The site of this town is unknown, but it was probably in northern India, which Alexander invaded in 326. Peritas' name is thought to come from the Macedonian word for "February" ("Perotius" in ancient Macedonian: the more familiar "Fevrou'arius" in modern Greek). This may have been the month in which the hound was born or acquired. Another source mentions the price paid by Alexander — a hundred "*minot*" — for a dog in India, name not mentioned.

At about this time Alexander also named a town, Bucephala, after his favourite horse, Bucephalus. This Thracian horse, about which more has been written than about Peritas, died in 326, three years before his young master's death at 33. The site of Bucephala has been identified "with a mound opposite the modern Jhelum" in Pakistan, south of Rawalpindi and near Kashmir.

About Alexander himself veritable mounds of volumes have been produced in both ancient and modern times. It could not have been otherwise, given the personality, the power, and the romance, and in the light of the stupendous battles and political history that he, and he alone directed in his brief life.

Alexander united Greece at the age of 21, occupied Egypt and founded Alexandria; he defeated Darius III, the mighty Persian emperor, and he "cut the Gordian Knot," to put the record in a very small capsule.

Alexander's story gave rise to scores of romances throughout the ancient world and during the Middle Ages, in places as far apart as England, Ethiopia, and Iceland. In a Persian version, he becomes a son of Darius; the Mohammedans make him a prophet, the Christians, an ascetic saint. Scholarly works have appeared on "*Le Type physique d'Alexandre le Grand*"; great artists painted him. Some of his qualities — "the high physical courage, the impulsive energy, the fervid imagination — stand out clearly. Beyond that, the disagreement begins."

Mosaic depiction of Alexander and his horse.

Alexander's education was entrusted to no less than the great Greek philosopher Aristotle, whom Philip brought to his court at Pella to educate his son, then 14. Aristotle, a student of Plato, was supposed to give the youth the "organic whole" of all Greek civilization. The young pupil was already mastering the arts of war; at 16, Alexander put down an uprising of hill tribes in Macedonia during his father's absence. (Aristotle once wrote, "poetry is . . . of higher value than history.")

Then came family troubles. Philip took a new wife, named Cleopatra, and sent Alexander's mother away — the usual story. Alexander went with his mother, and was never entirely reconciled to Philip, who was assassinated in 336. Alexander's mother, Olympias, was a princess from Epirus in Western Greece, which had sided with Macedonia against Rome. She is described as "of half-wild blood, weird, visionary and terrible."

In Babylon in the spring of 323, Alexander received delegations from all over the known world: he appeared superhuman, immortal. His last enterprise was to supervise the digging of a basin to contain 1,000 ships. On the 15th and 16th of June (?) he "caroused deep into the night." He developed a fever but took no notice. The fever grew worse. And then the entire Macedonian army, man by man, "passed through his chamber to bid him farewell." His end came on the 28th, after his probable, but at least much quoted saying: "I am dying with the help of too many physicians."

We may close with something definite, a couplet from Landor's "Regeneration":

The heart is hardest in the softest climes,
The passions flourish, the affections die.

Peritas, meet Pomero (q.v.).

PET — Dachshund who lived with, and then in a sense deserted, Liv Ullman, Norwegian stage and film actress, who has starred in roles ranging from Anne Frank to Hedda Gabler.

Ullman married and then divorced a young doctor to enter a stormy and difficult five-year relationship with famed Swedish director Ingmar Bergman, whom she never married but who fathered her daughter.

Pet may be the only female (bitch is not appropriate here) who in the end got the better of Bergman. She was very happy in her first home with Ullman's very pleasant young husband. Pet was "gentle and affectionate, loved to lie in his lap, and if she had been a cat she would have purred."

When this nice doctor-husband would return from work at the hospital, Pet would "yelp for joy" at the sound of his car . . . Then followed a feast of endearment between dog and man. At mealtimes, she lay at her master's feet to "look up at him adoringly."

How different it was when Ullman left her husband for the melancholy, self-centred Bergman. "The distrust was great on both sides," as Ullman continues this tale in her autobiography. When Bergman entered Pet's life,

> he attempted to bribe my friends to help him get rid of Pet. He asked them to take her into a street with heavy traffic, send her on to a final sleep at the veterinarian, leave her behind at the opposite end of town. But no one would.
>
> He and she chased each other wildly around my apartment. One of them kicked, the other bit. I was never again allowed to pat her or in any other way show her attention when *he* was there, and *she* growled when Ingmar took my hand.

When Ullman joined Bergman to live on a rocky island between Russia and Sweden, Pet came along as a very unwelcome guest. She was allowed to sleep in a small closet off the kitchen; the living room was out of bounds. "We had to steal our caresses when *he* was on the beach or in his study." But Pet, like a true dachshund, was not prepared to accept this as anything but temporary.

Analysing the situation, she "soon understood that it was best to give her love to the person who evidently was in command of her destiny." Slowly, she manipulated her way into the living room — "one yard a day, until finally she occupied a flattering position by the big open fireplace."

Never has a dog expressed such a degree of understanding as when Ingmar read aloud to me from a script. She looked dreamily into the air when his favourite records were being played. Her entire body quivered with longing when he put on his overcoat to take a walk, and she jumped for joy when she was finally given permission to go along, barking and bounding about in a violent demonstration, so that he would understand how important it was to take a watchdog along when strolling on the beach.

And in due course, the great Swedish director was making pronouncements along the lines of "Pet is an emotion on four legs."

When a baby girl was born to Ullman and Bergman — an event complicated by many pressures, professional, emotional, and others — Pet watched the infant sorrowfully. She lay under a sofa and came out only when the brand-new mother took the dog in her arms and scratched its stomach for as long as she had nursed the baby.

On one of her many quick trips to Hollywood, its weird ways viewed through innocently melancholy Nordic eyes, Ullman went to dinner at Hugh Hefner's, publisher of *Playboy*. Films were shown: "A dog makes love to a girl. I think of Pet and hope she will not discover what I am doing."

After five years of a doomed relationship, Ullman took her young daughter and left Bergman. Pet did not go with her. She and Bergman stood together at the doorway watching the two leave. "Pet sniffed at the ground," Ullman wrote of this well-remembered event, "so perhaps she was a bit ashamed of her betrayal."

PLADUMINI — Irrepressible dachshund of Max Liebermann (1847 – 1935), celebrated German painter who in his day painted most of Germany's VIP's. The son of strict Jewish parents, Liebermann was a cousin of Walther Rathenau, Germany's liberal Foreign Minister who was assassinated in 1922.

As a boy, Liebermann insisted on becoming a painter — and on loving animals. They appear in many of his works, including an adorable litter of suckling pigs. Young Liebermann attended the same school as the sons of Bismarck (*see* Tyras). Years later, the Bismarck boys wanted him to paint their father, and told him how "witty" the artist was. Liebermann decided against this attractive assignment, fearing he would be required to make jokes. Later he regretted the decision. (And after all, the two distinguished men could have talked about their dogs.)

Among the then celebrities painted by Liebermann are Albert Einstein, who was also a friend; Thomas Mann (*see* Bashan); Richard Strauss; Gerhardt Hauptmann; and several German Chancellors, including von Hindenburg, painted in 1927. The early Nazi movement was already furious that a Jew should paint the President. Liebermann's response: "What has painting to do with the fact that I am a Jew?"

Liebermann often discussed the question of Judaism with Einstein. His view, as reflected in these conversations, was: "All my life I have asked myself, what kind of human being are you? I never asked, are you a Jew, a Christian, or a Heathen? I was born a Jew and I will die a Jew."

In 1920 Liebermann became President of the Berlin Academy of Art. In 1933 he was ousted by the Nazis and his paintings were removed from all German museums. His elderly widow committed suicide in 1943 rather than be taken to a concentration camp. The Liebermann house in Berlin was looted, and all the paintings stolen and scattered.

In happier days, Pladumini the dachshund was usually on the sofa while the master worked, and was memorably present at artistic happenings. On one occasion in 1899, a jury was considering several hundred submitted paintings. Liebermann had brought his famous *Samson and Delilah* and was considering whether to submit it.

Pladumini, of course, came along too. An eye-witness recalled the event more than 50 years later, in meticulous Germanic detail, as a fitting vignette for the celebration of Liebermann's 80th birthday, in 1927:

> The jury was seriously debating every one of the many paintings, while the little dachshund was constantly scampering through the halls. He was in a fine mood — it was his "running day" — and he frolicked past the jury about every two minutes.
>
> Then Liebermann's large and impressive *Samson and Delilah* was brought in and placed on the floor against the wall. All the members of the jury stood solemnly before it.
>
> Just then the dachshund came racing past again. He slowed down and went over to Liebermann, who patted him.
>
> The dog then waddled calmly over to the huge painting and inspected it from one end to the other. At the corner of the frame he stopped, sniffed at the fresh oil and — can you imagine! — lifted his leg.
>
> A servant who was watching came at once with a crowbar to deal with the dachshund, enraged. The rest of us naturally were laughing.
>
> Liebermann said to the servant, "Ach, let the beast be. Who knows whether the critics will deal more nicely with the picture."

Liebermann's friend who recalled this episode at the birthday party pointed out the importance of the incident: it showed the painter's wisdom in being "resigned and indifferent" towards critics, while at the same time expressing great goodness towards all creatures.

But this is not the end of Pladumini's always forgiven mischief. It seems that this dachshund, who never suffered from the Prussian upbringing his master had received, killed some rabbits that belonged to the very servant at that jury meeting — the one who had come at him with a crowbar.

The servant demanded compensation for his rabbits. Liebermann, however, considered the "murderous impulse of his dachshund as its inalienable right." He overlooked all naughtiness in his "adorable doggie," and defended him against the servant "like a lion its young." Finally, though, just to cancel the notion that his dog might be considered "guilty," he gave the servant three marks — with a very sour expression.

Pladumini is still with us in Liebermann's paintings and sketches. For instance, there is the pastel study (1901) of the artist's daughter reading. Pladumini is for the moment safely at her feet, perhaps dreaming of spraying Samson, or of conquering rabbits.

In a drawing of a grandchild with the title *The Little Doggie Warms So Well* we see a dachshund cuddled on the bed next to

the child. (*See* Konrad Lorenz, in Jofi, for a similar disregard of the danger of germs.) A later dachshund, Männe, was sketched in 1918 "wanting to play" with a grand-daughter in the garden.

There are spaniels in Liebermann's huge output, and hunting dogs and German shepherds; lots of horses and goats, and those closely observed piglets, for whom the artist took home a piglet to study so he could draw the tiny animals correctly. Conspicuous by their absence are cats.

Liebermann's wife, whose end was so tragic, came from a well-established Berlin family; *her* mother was a committed suffragette. She was outspoken, sensible and charming, and sophisticated about art as well as germs.

Outspoken and witty (the Bismarck boys were absolutely right) in his strong Berlin accent, Liebermann's many sayings have been collected in several biographies. A typical comment about art: "When one looks at paintings by Franz Hals, it makes one want to paint. When one sees paintings by Rembrandt, it makes one want to stop."

POMERO and GIALLO — Walter Savage Landor's Pomeranians. Landor (1775—1864), English author best known for his *Imaginary Conversations*, has been described as "elaborate and of great charm." His verse is wide-ranging and of many moods. He was scholarly, like so many Victorian poets, but his terrible temper made for trouble throughout his life — except when he was playing with his beloved Pomeranians: interludes of bliss in a cantankerous career.

He attended Rugby, but was removed at the headmaster's request and tutored privately. He entered Trinity College at Oxford, where his "republican principles" led him to fire a gun "at the window of a Tory for whom he had an aversion." Expelled for the rest of the term, he refused to return although the authorities were ready to forgive him.

In 1808, aged 33, Landor left England for Spain to serve against Napolcon at the head of a regiment raised at his own expense (i.e., from money inherited from his father). The episode ended in disaster.

He married suddenly, in 1811, after falling "in love at first sight in a ballroom." Then followed years of wandering, brief periods at neglected estates where he tried to improve the land and "the wretchedness of the peasantry," quarrels with his wife, complete separation in 1835.

Landor was greatly admired by his friends, who included Browning (*see* Flush) and Swinburne, for the quality of his work, with its "noble and heroic pathos, subtle and tragic, profound and compassionate insight into character . . ." Landor wrote Latin verse, satires, elegies, epigrams.

He chose his dogs more wisely than his women. The small long-haired Pomeranian (bred from sled dogs used in Lapland and Iceland, but named after a German province) is described as "docile in temperament, vivacious in spirit, making it an 'adorable' pet, while its keen hearing and alertness make it an excellent watchdog."

So Landor, who had no children but loved them, enjoyed life with his dogs. All reference books refer to his terrible temper; but a very different account comes from an old friend who knew him when she was a child and often visited him at his cottage. She published her reminiscences nearly 30 years after his death, in 1891.

"There were few books in the house," she recalled, "but his massive brow a library in itself... We never saw his wife. Landor was fool enough to marry an utterly unsuitable wife while under the glamour of a pretty face..."

He was critical of the times: "People now want strong essences instead of flowers..." He liked Americans, but said he "could never live there because they have no cathedrals or painted glass." After much witty criticism, "he would unbend and talk nonsense with the youngest of us, but better still with Pomero, who in the absence of children — always dearly loved by Landor — was literally his playmate... (There were) explosive episodes of fun and frolic between noisy dog and no less noisy master."

Here is one of Landor's epigrams:

George the First was always reckoned
Vile, but viler George the Second;
And what mortal ever heard
Any good of George the Third?
When from earth the Fourth descended,
God be praised, the Georges ended!

On his 75 birthday, Landor produced this stately quatrain:

I strove with none, for none was worth my strife;
Nature I loved, and next to Nature, Art;
I warm'd both hands before the fire of Life,
It sinks; and I am ready to depart.

The reader is now in a position to substitute, if desired, two alternative final lines:

I played with Pomero and couldn't stand my wife:
My dogs were certainly the better part.

PRETIN — "Little Priest," small dog of Italian composer Giuseppe Verdi (1813 – 1901), so named because of Verdi's rampant anti-clericalism. Breed unknown; Pretin may have been a mixed breed, in line with his master's inclination towards free love.

A towering figure in opera, Verdi loved romantic love and the political cause of a united Italy. He composed such ever-popular operas as *Nabucco, Rigoletto, La Traviata, Aida,* and *Falstaff,* the last written and produced when he was 80.

The concluding words of *Falstaff,* sung to a fugue accompaniment, are "All the world's a joke." This may proclaim the gulf Verdi long felt between himself and his great adversary Richard Wagner (who was born the same year as Verdi, but who died eight years earlier).

Verdi's private life was anything but a joke. A recent 941-page biography underlines his "remarkable capacity for lust, love, disgust, anger and compassion." Verdi had many mistresses, fatal disputes with his parents, several illegitimate children, much trouble with censors — and pleasure from plenty of pets.

The themes of his many operas include jealousy, patricide, adultery, villainy, betrayal, and the family undermined by passion. Both his life and his work have been described as having "an almost overpowering vital force, restless and sometimes ruthless, at once humane and uncompromisingly brutal."

Pretin, however, enjoyed life with Verdi at the village of Busseto in the Duchy of Parma, Verdi's birthplace (Italy had not yet been born). Verdi's parents were innkeepers; Verdi played the organ in the local church at the age of 12, and composed his first symphony at the age of 15. To this village he returned in his later years, although very ambivalent towards its bourgeois pleasures, to live in relative quiet with his pet dogs and family. "Relative quiet" is the key term here: few musicians, as compared to writers and painters, seem to have kept dogs, so Pretin appears here with Verdi as an exception, though we know of no fugue in his honour.

Pretin and the other pets were less of a problem than Verdi's women. Here is the daughter of Verdi's teacher, whom he courted when he was 21 and while engaged to marry the daughter of his patron: "I pray to God that I may forget him forever."

Here is Verdi 37 years later, on the "new" world of music, just before the triumphant gala opening of *Aida* in Cairo. The opera had been composed at the invitation of Ismail Pasha, ruler of Egypt, to celebrate the completion of the Suez Canal. Verdi refused to attend. Instead, he wrote to an Italian journalist in Cairo:

In these days art is no longer art, but a trade ... (for which) you must achieve, if not success, notoriety at any price!

In my early days it was always a pleasure to come before the public with my operas, almost friendless and without a lot of preliminary chatter or influence, and stand up to be shot at; and I was delighted if I succeeded in creating a favourable impression.

But now, what a fuss is made about an opera! Journalists, singers, directors, professors of music and the rest must all contribute their stone to the temple of publicity, to build a cornice out of wretched tittle-tattle that adds nothing to the worth of an opera ... It is deplorable, absolutely deplorable.

QUOODLE — Dog (breed unknown) acquired by Gilbert Keith Chesterton (1874 – 1936) in his middle years. Chesterton, essayist, novelist, poet, a convert to Catholicism, reacted against 19th century materialism, and championed any number of lost causes with finesse and brilliance. His writings cover a wide range of moral and social criticism, often with fantasy and humour and in the form of aphoristic paradoxes. His *Father Brown* detective series earned him the largest audience.

For his dog, Chesterton wrote in *The Song of Quoodle*:

> *They haven't got no noses,*
> *The fallen sons of Eve . . .*
> *And goodness only knowses*
> *The Noselessness of Man.*

London-born Chesterton was deprived of the pleasure of growing up with a dog. At St Paul's school he won the "Milton" prize for English verse at an unusually early age. He studied at London's Slade School of Art and became a competent draghtsman, but literature soon took over, starting with journalistic articles in revolt against Victorian complacency in an "unconventional, swash-buckling and dogmatic" style.

His much-praised critical essays include works on Browning (*see* Flush), Carlyle (*see* Nero) and Hardy (*see* Wessie), of whom he wrote,

Hardy went down to botanize in the swamp, (and) . . . became a sort of village atheist brooding and blaspheming over the village idiot.

In an essay "On the Pleasures of No Longer Being Very Young," published in 1931 when he was 57, Chesterton tells us that "it is great fun to find out that the world has not repeated proverbs because they are proverbial, but because they are practical."

Until I owned a dog, I never knew what was meant by the proverb about letting a sleeping dog lie, or the fable about the dog in the manger. Now those dead phrases are quite alive to me, for they are parts of a perfectly practical psychology.

(Those who have always lived with dogs might not accept this literary precept, and might not consider such psychological rules as inevitably true.)

Elsewhere in this essay, Chesterton makes more widely acceptable the differences between youth and non-youth:

Another paradox is this: that it is not the young people who realize the new world. The moderns do not realize modernity. They have never known anything else . . .

The older generation consists of those who do remember (another) time . . . They feel sharply and clearly the epoch which is beginning, for they were there before it began.

From *The Wisdom of Father Brown*: "Journalism largely consists in saying 'Lord Jones is dead' to people who never knew Lord Jones was alive."

From *The Innocence of Father Brown*: "To be clever enough to get all that money, one must be stupid enough to want it."

And from some of the poetry:

> *The villas and the chapels where*
> *I learned with little labour*
> *The way to love my fellow-man*
> *And hate my next-door neighbour.*

In *The Donkey*, that poor beast is described as having a "monstrous head and sickening cry, ears like errant wings / The devil's walking parody / On all four-footed things." But Chesterton, who also wrote about St Francis of Assisi, manages to give the donkey his due, his great theological moment:

Fools! For I also had my hour;
One far fierce hour and sweet:
There was a shout about my ears,
And palms before my feet.

ROB ROY — White collie belonging to Calvin Coolidge (1872–1933), 30th President of the United States, and one of a record list of presidential pets. A beautiful portrait of Rob Roy, painted by Howard Chandler Christy (he painted many famous personalities, including Mussolini), hangs in the White House in Washington, D.C. It shows the once famous presidential collie gazing admiringly at elegant Mrs Coolidge, the former Grace Anne Goodhue, whom the President-to-be married in 1905 when he was still only a local Republican leader in Massachusetts.

Rob Roy was by no means this popular President's only collie. The others were Bessie, Foxy, Mule Ears (what a name), Oshkosh, and Prudence Prim. Then there were the chow chows — Blackberry, Ruby Rough, and Tiny Tim. Boston Beans was the bulldog; Calamity Jane, Jolly Jane, and Diana were the Shetland sheep dogs. King Kole was the Belgian police dog, Laddie Buck and Paul Pry were Airedales, and Peter Pan the wire-haired fox terrier. What a canine collection, surely deserving some presidential prize! And that is still not all. Coolidge, often described as "taciturn," obviously loved all living things, and we may be sure there were interesting conversations with his other apolitical friends. Besides his dogs, these included four cats; the raccoons Horace and Rebecca; Smoky the bobcat, Enoch the goose, Ebenezer the donkey, Nip and Snowflake the canaries, and Old Bill, the thrush.

After this dazzling list, we return to Rob Roy Coolidge, who was named after Rob Roy MacGregor, a "singular" Scotsman in the novel of that name by Sir Walter Scott. His story is a bit more adventurous and thickly-plotted than the life of the President.

Coolidge, born in Plymouth, Vermont, served two terms. As

Vice-President, he succeeded to the presidency on the death of Harding and served from 1921 to 1923. In 1924 he was re-elected and served from 1925 to 1929, having the luck to leave just before the Great Depression that hit his successor, Herbert Hoover.

In the history books, Cleveland is recalled as a "poor mixer," shy, taciturn, and apparently cold (except, as is rarely made clear, with Bessie, Blackberry, Blaze, et al.) but as having shrewd, dry political sense. He was known for such statements as "The business of America is business," and "In politics we need more of the office desk and less of the show window." And "the man who builds a factory builds a temple."

As Governor of Massachusetts, his most remembered act was to call out the state guard to break the Boston police strike. The voters admired his thrift, and his policies of obedience to law, religious tolerance — and of saying what he meant. ("Down, Rob Roy.")

Alice Roosevelt Longworth, of the old Washington scene, remarked that "he had been weaned on a dill pickle." And as H. L. Mencken put it, "He slept more than any other President . . . Nero fiddled, but Coolidge only snored."

Rob Roy Coolidge's ancestors came from thrifty, hard-working Scotland, where they earned their keep as keenly intelligent herding dogs. Their presidential descendant lived in the elegant White House, posed for his portrait, and did not suffer from frugality as much as did human guests.

Or so goes the story from then super-celebrity comedian Will Rogers. Invited to a White House dinner, Will Rogers became annoyed that great helpings of food were being passed down to the assembled waiting dogs — Bessy, Foxy, R.R. et al. — while the human guests were getting very little. Finally, Rogers did what only he could do: got down on all fours and started barking.

RUFUS — Poodle and painting companion of Winston Churchill (1874 – 1965), British statesman, soldier, author of histories, biographies, memoirs. Churchill won the Nobel Prize for literature in 1953, the same year he was knighted.

So much has been written by and about Churchill that his poodle has, somehow, fallen through the cracks. Fortunately, Winnie and Rufus are immortalized in a marvellous photograph by Phillipe Halsman of the two in splendid solitude in 1951 at Chartwell.

"Eventually he reached the end of the garden," Halsman wrote of this estimable photo encounter, "and sat down on a small rock. His poodle Rufus installed himself behind Churchill's back."

A year earlier, during the election campaign of 1950, when Churchill was out of office and had become leader of the Conservative opposition, he was photographed with another dog. The campaign was successful, and Churchill led the Conservative Party to victory that year. No Rufus, and the photographer is unknown. The dog in the photo is described as "his," and it is a bulldog; no name given. Perhaps a poodle would have been considered too effete, too non-British.

Certainly this bulldog, phlegmatic-looking but pleasant, is the proper public symbol for John Bull's Island and for the Rt. Hon. Sir Winston Spencer Churchill, its most famous, most courageous leader. The bulldog, in any case, stands placidly on a chair so that cigar-smoking Winnie can stroke its head for his dog-loving audience. But somebody else is holding the leash.

Churchill was ahead of his time in seeing the Nazi danger, and his career was unparalleled, although as a boy he was an undistinguished student. (A result, the psycho-historian might say, of an unfortunate relationship with his father, and of unrequited love for his mother.) His friendship with President Roosevelt (*see* Fala) was deep and mutual. On FDR's death, Churchill wrote:

In Franklin Roosevelt there died the greatest American friend we have ever known, and the greatest champion of freedom who has ever brought help and comfort from the New World to the Old.

Churchill and bulldog at election time. Rufus at home.

"Winnie" was wrong on several political issues and made some calamitous mistakes. But no orator matched his speeches, and few statesmen have been so quotable. He is said to have had a speech defect early in his career and consulted an expert for help: "I can't go through life looking for words with no S."

His post–Victorian optimism (though he also suffered bouts of melancholy) make some of his comments sound quaint today, to put it mildly. In his essay on King George V, published in 1937, he wrote: "The thriving free press has become a faithful guardian of the Royal Family." (*See* Harris.)

But who can match — quite aside from the oft-quoted ones that echo in the mind — the well-turned witticisms:

If Hitler invaded Hell, I would make at least a favourable reference to the Devil in the House of Commons.

Nothing in war ever goes right except by accident.

I am ready to meet my Maker. Whether my Maker is prepared for the great ordeal of meeting me is another matter.

"SALVARSAN" — Dachshund who went everywhere with his master Professor Paul Ehrlich (1854 – 1915), Nobel Prize-winning German-Jewish medical researcher, biochemist, bacteriologist, pioneer of modern immunology and chemotherapy.

With a team of researchers, Ehrlich discovered — as an unexpected outcome of research into sleeping sickness — the treatment for syphilis in 1909. A year earlier, he had shared (with Metchnikoff, Pasteur's successor) the Nobel Prize for medicine and physiology. The arsenic compound "606" (Salvarsan) was so named because it was the 606th trial made by Ehrlich and his Japanese assistants. It became the specific treatment for the venereal disease, then considered more hopeless than AIDS is today; like AIDS, it was thought in some circles to be divine punishment for sin. Later, Ehrlich also worked on the cancer problem, but finally admitted "Cancer is too hard."

The film *The Story of Dr Ehrlich's Magic Bullet*, in which Ehrlich was played by Edward G. Robinson, presented a rather romantic account of the discovery. Produced by Warner Bros., it was named one of the ten best films of 1941.

Ehrlich was ahead of his time in many ways — including his high evaluation of able professional women and his unqualified willingness to work with them. At the same time, he was not one for spending hours at his laboratory: he rarely arrived there before ten in the morning — with his dachshund — and was usually at home by early afternoon, to spend time with his wife — and dachshund. Much of his work was done in his head, and the subsequent long laboratory tests were to confirm his mental, theoretical work.

Although he worked with laboratory animals, Ehrlich was

known for his kindness to animals in general. He kept a pet toad in his garden, always saw to its food — and predicted changes in weather by its behaviour.

In 1913, two years before his death and one year before the outbreak of WWI (Ehrlich, like so many German Jews, was a confirmed German nationalist), he was visited in Frankfurt by Chaim Weizmann, who 35 years later was to become the first President of the State of Israel.

No dachshund appears in Weizmann's description of the meeting in his memoirs, although there are mice and rabbits (in laboratory cages). Weizmann, unlike affluent, early-Westernized Ehrlich, spent his early poverty-stricken years in Russia, where Jewish villagers had no time to develop canine interests.

But their meeting is worth retrieving — it was unforgettable for Weizmann — because of its picture of Ehrlich at the height of his fame. Weizmann, trained in chemistry, wanted to discuss Zionism and nothing else. He knew it would be very difficult to even arrange an appointment with the great man; he managed it through the good offices of a professor friend who was related to Mrs Ehrlich. This friend, Weizmann wrote in his memoirs, was very doubtful that Ehrlich "would give me five minutes of his time . . . for Ehrlich was utterly impervious to outside influences, especially in his laboratory." Yet in the end, it was an "extraordinary" interview. Weizmann writes:

I have retained an ineradicable impression of Ehrlich. His figure was small and stocky, but he had a head of great beauty, delicately chiselled; and out of his face looked a pair of eyes which were the most penetrating that I have ever seen — but they were eyes filled with human kindness.

He introduced me to some of his assistants; and especially to his rabbits and guinea pigs . . . He spoke of chemistry as of a weapon with which one could shoot at diseases: if you have your chemistry properly applied, you can aim straight at the cause of a sickness.

At the end of the laboratory tour (the dog presumably at their heels) and after Weizmann finally had the courage to bring up the subject of Zionism, Ehrlich invited him to come to his home that night, adding pleasantly:

You have kept me nearly an hour. Do you know that out there, in the corridor, there are counts, princes and ministers who are waiting to see me, and who will be happy if I give them ten minutes of my time?

To which Weizmann, never at a loss for words, replied, "Yes, Professor Ehrlich, but the difference between me and your other visitors is that they come to receive an injection from you, but I came to give you one."

That night at the Ehrlich's pleasant Frankfurt house, Weiz-

mann again mentions no dachshund, though one was surely present. He describes Mrs E. as a "typical sweet German *Hausfrau*, who was always scolding her husband for his untidiness and for his ceaseless smoking." Ehrlich was never without a cigar, and W. believed that this led to his early death.

Shortly after this meeting, W. learned that he had won over Ehrlich, and he became an enthusiastic member of the Committee for the Hebrew University in Jerusalem. But of course, W. was not won over to the canine cause.

Ehrlich had many enemies (as is the case in most professions), and many of his theories were ridiculed at the time. Salvarsan had no enemies; in fact he surely had other dachshund friends on that pleasant Frankfurt street. When the Nazis came to power, Ehrlich's name was removed from the Frankfurt street previously named in his honour; after the Nazi defeat, Ehrlich's name was restored to the street. Our illustration shows a nice little German girl walking to her home on Ehrlich Street with her dachshund. A relative of Ehrlich's dog? In any case surely an acquaintance on "Sandhof Str.," later Ehrlich Str., then back to Sandhof Str., and finally again to Ehrlich Str. The little girl grew up, married an artist, and came to Israel. From a water-colour.

SARAH   West Highland terrier who lived, and slept, with Sir Alfred Hitchcock (1899–1980) and his wife in Bel Air, California. Sarah had a special pillow on the bed between the Hitchcocks.

At a breakfast photo-opportunity with Sarah, the great film director, who created such classics as *The Lady Vanishes* and *The Thirty-Nine Steps*, informed photographer Phillipe Halsman that he was delighted that he, his wife, and their dog celebrated their birthdays on three consecutive days — August 12, 13, and 14.

This photo, taken when Sir Alfred was 75 and Sarah two-and-a-half, shows the director glancing haughtily at the morning paper; Sarah, just behind him, also evaluates the headline. There is just one cup of coffee. The year was 1974, two years after *Frenzy* and two years before Hitchcock's last film, *Family Plot*.

The son of a London poultry dealer, Hitchcock attended a Jesuit school, studied engineering at the University of London, and entered the young film industry as a designer of title cards for silent movies. He directed his first film at the age of 26, his first thriller at 27, and England's first successful talking picture, *Blackmail*, in 1929.

He left England for Hollywood in 1938 and his first American film, *Rebecca*, won the Academy Award for best picture. He was soon the crowned king of directors, with a name that in itself attracted the public as much as any star's. As all film addicts know, the suspense master's classic films include *The Lady Vanishes*, *Lifeboat*, *Spellbound*, *Dial M for Murder*, *Rear Window*, and *To Catch a Thief*.

In the Fifties and Sixties he took on TV with several series that he introduced and occasionally directed.

SHADOW — Favourite hound of Elizabeth, Empress of Austria and Queen of Hungary (1837 — 98).

Elizabeth Amelie Eugenie, one of the 15 children of Duke Maximilian Joseph of Bavaria, was considered the most beautiful princess in Europe when, at 16, she met Emperor Franz Joseph of

Austria. He fell in love with her on sight, and they were married a year later, in 1854.

Elizabeth was not only beautiful, but intelligent and the product of an "unconventional" upbringing. Her "eccentric" father took her along on hunting expeditions and she became an expert rider and rock climber. All this with "golden-brown hair a yard long, a floating walk, sparkling moods — and great melancholy."

She was interested in art and architecture, disliked publicity, and built a palace in the Greek style at Corfu. Although she tended to prefer the Hungarians, she was popular with the Austrians for her charitable behaviour, as when she cared for the wounded in the Austro-Prussian War of 1866.

The following year, a beautiful photograph was taken of her and "Shadow" — not out in the field preparing for the hunt, but in a very well-appointed salon: Elizabeth on a sofa and Shadow at her feet on the rug. This hound was not relegated to the kennels, however royal.

At the time this scene was photographed, the couple's child, Prince Rudolf of Hapsburg, was a boy of ten. Naturally, great hopes were centred on the crown prince. His father stressed his military education, but his natural interests were very different: literature, natural history, and in due course, girls. He made no secret of his free-thinking, anti-clerical views. He was married in 1881 to the Princess of Belgium, but developed a passion for a beautiful young baroness. In January 1889, the bodies of the two lovers were found at Rudolf's hunting lodge at Mayerling. Rumours and theories occupied everyone; the truth was never discovered.

The tragic death of her son was a shock from which Elizabeth never recovered. And there were other terrible tragedies. Her cousin Ludwig II of Bavaria ("handsome, gifted, liberal, with a prodigality and eccentricity that developed into incurable insanity") committed suicide by drowning, and forced his physician to share his death.

Her husband's brother, Maximilian, was killed by firing squad in Mexico. Her sister died in a fire at a charity bazaar in Paris. "I long for death," Elizabeth wrote her daughter, four months before she found it in Switzerland. Meanwhile, she took lessons in the most dangerous tricks of circus-riding, walked and hunted recklessly, dieted to excess (one orange or a glass of milk a day).

Anarchism and assassination were in the air at the close of the last century. On September 9, 1898, Elizabeth and her lady-in-waiting were walking from her hotel at Geneva after visiting the fairyland villa of Baroness Adolfe de Rothschild (tame miniature porcupines from Java, exotic coloured birds in the private park). Near the hotel, she was fatally stabbed by an Italian anarchist, Luigi Luccheni. (He had grown up in a poorhouse, and gone to work as a day labourer at the age of nine. It was an age of extremes.)

Luigi was delighted when he heard that the Empress was dead. Since there is no death penalty in Switzerland, he was sentenced to life imprisonment; 12 years later, after a quarrel with the warder, he hanged himself with his belt.

The romantic and tragic stories of Elizabeth and her son, Prince Rudolf, are well known to those educated in Austria. Many others know them best through an old movie, *Mayerling*, in which Rudolf was played by Charles Boyer. That events may cast their "Shadows" into the future may be read into the incredible fact that Boyer's only child, a son, died in a mysterious suicide.

Readers preferring gossip to romantic echoes might wish to consult *Martyrdom of an Empress*, published anonymously in 1899 and containing plenty of juicy court tittle-tattle.

Of this assessment of her, by the then Queen of Romania: she was "a fairies' child, with hidden wings, who flies away whenever she finds the world unbearable." And her "Shadow" inadequate.

"TOBI" — Small dog of Tobit and his son Tobias, who travelled on a marvellous adventure with a happy ending, guided by the angel Raphael. These and other characters appear in the *Book of Tobit*, probably the earliest of the books of the Apocrypha. Often called a "religious novel" and cheerfully didactic in tone, its date, after much scholarly controversy, is thought to be around 250 B.C. The books of the Apocrypha — *Judith, Bel and the Dragon*, the *Maccabees* and others — are within the Catholic canon; in the Protestant Bible they are "recommended as useful and as good reading" but are not part of the Holy Scriptures.

They are completely out of the Jewish Bible, and known as "extraneous books." The author, however, is thought to have been an Egyptian Jew writing in Aramaic or Greek and using many elements from earlier religions.

Tobi — his name was applied much later; in the story he has none and is known as "little dog" — came to be popular because of his appeal to many artists. Rembrandt (1606 – 69), for instance, puts little Tobi into nearly all the many sketches and etchings he did for the story of Tobias, apparently one of his favourites.

The plot, very uplifting but yet a good read, has the right elements — faith and charity, a curse, romance, two young lovers, distant but intended for each other (both, oddly enough, apparently Only Children), a long voyage, an angel, a miracle — and that little dog.

The story, in brief: Tobias, a pious Jew who follows all the commandments, was originally from Galilee but had been taken into captivity in Assyria, where he bravely defied all pagan opposition to Jewish tradition: for instance, he insisted on burying corpses. His wife Hannah tended to be shrewish. Their only child was a boy, Tobias, nicknamed Tobit.

One day Tobias the father was blinded when a bird flying overhead dropped some "filth" in his eye. Now misfortune and poverty befell the family, but Tobias bore it all bravely, saying that we are all God's children and await the life He gives us.

Meanwhile, far off in a distant land, Sarah, the daughter of a family relative, was also having a hard time: seven, yes seven of her newly-wedded husbands had died right after the marriage: the evil spirit Asmodi had killed them at just the crucial moment. But Sarah, too, firm in her belief, prayed to God in much the same way as Tobias was doing at that very same instant.

Tobias, thinking he was about to die, decided to send his son on a long voyage to his relative, who actually owed him some money. He told his son that, although he was poor, he must always share what he had with those in need, along the route, and that God would surely provide for those who served him truly.

Young Tobias had no idea how he was going to accomplish all that his father wanted. But as soon as he left the house, accompanied by his little dog, he met a stranger outside who told him not to worry. "I am an Israelite," said the unknown young man, "and I will take you where you are going and bring you safely home."

How could Tobias know that this was the angel Raphael?

While crossing the Tigris River they caught a fish, and the stranger told Tobias to take with them the heart and the liver; they ate the rest. Finally, they arrive at their relatives' house. And in due course Tobias is married to Sarah, and the curse is lifted. And then they make the long voyage home, and the blind Tobias goes to the door. And here, a rare jewel in ancient Jewish writing, "the little dog runs ahead wagging his tail, jumped about and was very happy."

Then Sarah arrives with a camel caravan full of riches, and everybody lives happily ever after. In fact, as the book states, Old Tobias lives until the age of 102, and his son to 99. And all their children were good and God-fearing.

One of Rembrandt's sketches of Tobi, here returning home.

The little dog's next immortalization, in a very different style, happened around 1840. It was then that he received the name "Tobi," and became a trained dog in the English children's Punch and Judy puppet shows. But here Punch is "cruel and boastful," and his wife Judy, "faithless."

Why was this fine story excluded from the Jewish Scriptures? Anybody's guess will do; one theory might well be the curious and very non-Jewish presence of the dog. Indeed, some experts claim that elements in *Tobit* may be traced to "magical" traditions of the early Persian religion, particularly Zoroaster (*see* "Zodi").

The Tobit story, it is pointed out, contemplates a return of the Jews to their country but it is a purely nationalist return, with no trace of a personal Messiah. And nowhere else have we "so complete and beautiful a picture of the domestic life of the Jews (after the First Return). Almost every family relation (and pet!) is touched upon, with natural grace and affection." Fragments of the *Tobit* book were found among the Dead Sea Scrolls.

In any event, few small dogs have travelled as far — and as long — as this one.

TONY — Full name, George Washington. Agatha Christie's Yorkshire terrier, the first of many dogs in her life (1891 – 1976).

On her fifth birthday, in 1896, Agatha Christie — who was to become, to her surprise, a world celebrity as a mystery writer — received a four-month-old puppy from her doting parents. "It was the most shattering thing that ever happened to me," she wrote with perfect recall 70 years later. "Such unbelievable joy that I was unable to say a word."

Struck dumb by the magnitude of her bliss, she retired without a sound to the lavatory, selected as being "a perfect place for meditation. I closed the heavy mahogany shelf-like seat, gazed unseeingly at the map of Torquay that hung on the wall, and gave myself up to realization":

I have a dog...a dog...It's a dog of my own...my very own dog... It's a Yorkshire terrier . . . my dog . . . My very own dog . . .

Agatha's mother told her later that her father had been disappointed by the way she reacted to the gift. He had been sure she would love it; instead, "She doesn't seem to care about it at all." Agatha's more understanding mother explained that the little girl simply needed more time: "She can't quite take it in yet."

Young George "Tony" Washington found himself in a small, idyllic, middle-class, rural world. Agatha was enjoying a happy Victorian childhood in an English country home — older brother and sister away at school, devoted parents, a Nannie of her own ("the outstanding figure in my early life"), cooks and maids. Highly imaginative, she had taught herself to read at four, which was against the educational theories of the moment. So the embarrassed nurse, finding her charge one day reading a book called *The Angel of Love*, announced apologetically to the mother, "I'm afraid, Ma'am, that Miss Agatha can *read.*"

"My mother was distressed, but there it was. From then on, for Christmas and birthdays, I demanded books."

Before the arrival of Tony the dog, there was a much-loved canary, Goldie. On one starkly dramatic occasion, Goldie was thought to have flown out the window. But, it turned out, he had

been in the room all day, on the curtain pole. It was the kind of event Agatha never forgot.

She also played a secret game of "Kittens," of which she was one — there were five little cats, and their mother's name was "Mrs Benson." Captain Benson, the kittens' father, had been lost at sea and the family was "left in penury." A promisingly perfect childhood for an inventive writer of countless plots. And one who remained modest throughout, considering herself "lowbrow" and simply blessed by luck and by love, from men and beasts.

Tony the terrier soon became a member of a new "Secret Saga" plotted by Agatha. "We were both shy and made only tentative advances to each other. But by the end of the week Tony and I were inseparable . . . he was good-natured, affectionate, and lent himself to all my fancies . . ."

Her autobiography was written at an archaeological site; she recalls finding a little dog buried under an ancient threshold, under a clay slab inscribed with the words, *"Don't stop to think, Bite him!"* Such a good motto for a guard dog, muses Agatha: "You can see it being written on the clay, and someone laughing."

At the close of her autobiography, written when she was 75, Agatha Christie lists the memories closest to her. The very last, the "most poignant of experiences — Goldie the canary hopping down from the curtain pole after a day of hopeless despair." Not the day Tony arrived: that was not "poignant" and there had been no despair, but was the first of many "true friendships" to come. For Agatha's earliest imaginary playmates also included the children of "Mrs Green" — called Poodle, Squirrel and Tree. "They were not quite children and not quite dogs, but intermediate creatures between the two." A concept worth studying by anyone wishing to write the longest-running play of all time — as in the case of Agatha Christie's *The Mousetrap*, which opened in 1952 and passed its 18,000th performance in February 1996.

Young Agatha, young Tony, Victorian father, in garden.

TRUMP — Pug dog, much loved and much painted by William Hogarth (1697—1764), English painter and engraver. Hogarth, regarded as the supreme political satirist, has also been called "the most English English artist that ever lived." His long involvement with pugs may reflect his belief that there was some "innate connection" between pug dogs (rather than bulldogs) and Englishmen.

The pug has in fact been seen as a miniature bulldog (as Hogarth himself, if only physically, was a small-scale Englishman; see below). But some sources also trace the pug back to 400 B.C., and believe it was bred to be a companion to Buddhist monks in Tibet.

Never justly appreciated during his lifetime — he was too cantankerous and too critical of hypocrisy and stupidity — Hogarth's great acclaim came a century after his death, and Trump and his fellow-pugs live on in galleries and collections.

He was perhaps most ahead of his time in attacking cruelty to animals. In *The Four Stages of Cruelty*, painted in 1751, the artist said that his aim was

> to correct that barbarous treatment of animals, the very sight of which renders the streets of our metropolis so distressing to every feeling mind. I am more proud of having been the author (of these prints) than I should be of having painted Raphael's works.

Hogarth's pictures were filled with morality and with stories. He liked to consider himself an author rather than an artist: "I have endeavoured," he said, "to treat my subject as a dramatic writer; my picture is my stage, and men and women my players." He attacked injustice, corruption, the wages of sin, and the dire conditions of London's poor; his *Rake's Progress* became an opera by Stravinsky, with libretto by Auden. In *Gin Lane* and *Beer Street*, he contrasted "the dreadful consequences of gin-drinking . . . with the wholesome effects of beer."

Trump, just one of Hogarth's several pugs, is the one immortalized in a famous self-portrait of the artist painted in 1745 which also involved the nature of aesthetics (see below).

Vulcan was another of the artist's pugs, and records show that he acquired his first pug in 1730. Hogarth had a long and special affection for this small, decisive-looking dog, the largest of the toy breeds. The artist himself, for a brief nod to psycho-aesthetics, was barely five feet tall, but always carried a sword "and took no nonsense from anyone."

Hogarth was anti-French and patriotically English. But he pictured England with all her sins and all the tragedies of the time: prison, poverty, debts, harsh and endless work for the lower classes. The French, he thought, had corrupted England with aristocratic airs and frippery. He was pro-Dutch in the tensions between the Dutch and the French, and identified Dutch interests with those of England: hence his description of pugnacious little pugs as "Dutch dogs," for having "dogged" determination and independent spirit. The Dutch Republic, in Hogarth's view, was the home of freedom, toleration, social equality and intellectual progress, while France had an abolute monarchy and the Church.

Hogarth's *March of the Guards toward Scotland* was painted in 1745, the year of Bonnie Prince Charlie's doomed attempt to overthrow the Hanoverian dynasty (*see* "Bonny"). Hogarth wanted to dedicate his painting to King George II, but the King hated it and thought the artist should be imprisoned. So Hogarth instead dedicated it to Frederick the Great (*see* Alcmene) whom he admired as a monarch who encouraged the arts and sciences.

In a painting of the Strode family in 1738, a pug on one side of the room gazes with calm contempt at a Frenchified dog on the other. In another painting, *Captain Lord George Graham in His Cabin*, the (ever-present) pug is wearing a wig to make fun of French foppishness and ostentation. And in his series of satirical engravings, *Marriage à la Mode*, there are dogs in nearly every scene — behaving far better than the upper classes are depicted in their private lives.

The self-portrait with Trump is also part of the ever-continuing mystification of art criticism and its experts. On the painter's palette is a serpentine line with the inscription, "The Line of Beauty, W.H. 1745." What on earth did this mean? The puzzle

aroused much interest and interpretation. Hogarth said later that he had painted it to find out whether other artists and "connoisseurs" had any real idea as to what made a picture "beautiful." The "bait soon took," as Hogarth said, "and no Egyptian hieroglyphic ever amused more than it did for a time," with painters and sculptors searching for the explanation.

To provide it, and to deal with "the fluctuating ideas of Taste," Hogarth published a treatise, his "Analysis of Beauty," in 1753. In it, with due deference to Michelangelo's precept that a figure should always be "Pyramidal, Serpent-like, and multiplied by one, two, and three," Hogarth defined the serpentine line on his palette as the line formed by "winding a wire in even progression around a cone." Such a line, he believed, was not only the secret of beauty "but also the movement of life." Hogarth's friends saw this as the final word on the subject; his enemies considered it nonsense.

But would not every pug today realize that Hogarth's mysterious serpentine line becomes — when doubled, and in three dimensions — no less than the Double Helix of modern science, which does indeed lead, so it is believed in the best circles, to the secret of life?

Pugs today in any case continue to live in the best circles. More than 400 canine generations after Trump and Victor, modern readers were able to meet Bingo and Violet, two pugs owned by bestselling writer Elizabeth Marshall Thomas, dog-behaviour analyst, anthropologist and novelist. Bingo would have enchanted Hogarth: he was brave, friendly, forthright, enterprising, and intelligent. Violet, unfortunately, was none of these. She had been bred for show and had impressive registration papers; as a result she became a "dithering, hyper-excited adult" with frequent episodes of panic. These, Ms Thomas realized too late, were caused by her overly-high breeding, which made Violet more deformed than Bingo — so essential today in the show ring. In dogs like pugs, Pekingese and others that are required to have "gruesomely foreshortened faces," all the necessary organs are "squashed together" inside the deformed skull. So poor little

Violet often collapsed in convulsions and could hardly be trained.

Trump, in his portrait, does not look at all "gruesomely foreshortened," and his nose is of quite "normal" length. He was never intended for show — except today, in galleries.

This is a beautifully documented example of how modern show dogs often fall far short of their ancient ancestors in character and health. Animal behaviourist Konrad Lorenz illustrates the point with great emotion regarding chows (*see* Jofi).

Hogarth's life was beset by enemies, by arguments over both money and principles, and by plenty of bitter human dog-fights. His modern reputation began when Whistler proclaimed that Hogarth was "the only great English painter." As a social force in his medium and as a pugnacious friend of all animals, he has never been surpassed.

(above) From Marriage à la Mode *engravings; pug in place at right.*

TYRAS — Huge amber-eyed black dog, companion of Prince Otto von Bismarck (1815 – 98).

The life and times of the "Iron Chancellor" are still easily available in any history book. Bismarck was appointed Prime Minister of Prussia, made war against Denmark and Austria; became Chancellor of the North German Federation; was victorious in the Franco-Prussian War, and became first Chancellor of the German Empire, constituted in 1871. And finally, after the exercise of much power at the summit under Emperor William I, was forced to resign in 1890 by the new Emperor, William II.

It is therefore a pleasure to provide the following little-known scene from the family life of Bismarck, his wife Joanna, to whom he was deeply devoted (and wrote seven published volumes of letters), and of big black Tyras.

The time is October 7, 1889, at "Friedrichsruh," the isolated family castle in Saxony. Emperor William I, whom Bismarck served loyally, had died the previous year in March at the age of 91. Bismarck is not happy in his dealings with William II (who was to lead his country into the disaster of WWI).

It is breakfast time at the castle. A visitor has arrived to show Bismarck a much-discussed marvellous new invention — a Talking Machine, later to become the phonograph! According to a detailed account of this morning's events, Bismarck, in his old-fashioned frock-coat with white stock in place of tie, carefully wipes the last bit of egg-yolk from his mustache and announces, "Now I would like to meet the famous new machine, which it is said, can speak and play music."

He and Joanna and Tyras move from the breakfast room to the salon, where the famous Apparatus sits on a little table.

"If Your Gracious Highness would permit," says the Hamburg representative of the American Trading Company, "we will first hear the *Radetsky March* which the musicians of the Kaiser Franz Regiment played for us recently."

Tyras, at Bismarck's feet, follows with alert amber eyes every motion of the "phonograph-man" as the cylinders are changed.

(overleaf) Prince Bismarck's Dream, *cartoon in Russian journal, 1891.*

Now comes the voice of soprano Lilli Lehmann singing an aria from *Norma*! The dog pricks up his ears and begins to growl threateningly.

"Quiet, Tyras," says his master's voice. (*See* Nipper.) "You are a *Banause*!" (The conversation was, of course, in German, though Bismarck spoke excellent French and knew English.) And what does *Banause* mean? It comes from the Greek, and means uncouth yokel, uneducated peasant.

Back to the castle. After a few more scratchy songs, Bismarck expresses the wish to try his own voice via the new-fangled machine. And so, first in a clear high voice, he sings a waltz. Then the Iron Chancellor relates a few sentences from the history of Emperor Frederick Barbarossa's Crusade to the Holy Land. Finally, he sings *Gaudeamus Igitur*. All this is heard and recorded by the new machine, and of course by Tyras. And as the first notes of the old (Latin) students' song ring through the room of the castle, the big dog raises himself from his nook, lumbers over to Bismarck, and rubs his head against the Chancellor's knee.

Bismarck, who had studied law and read widely in philosophy, had "an astonishing knowledge of literature." And what does the name "Tyras" mean? One definition would be the ancient Greek name for the river Dnieper in Russia.

The nature of Bismarck's role, though never his importance, has often been revised by historians. No revision need be made of his many pronouncements, including one of the most famous: "Politics is no exact science."

Or, as the reader now knows: "Tyras, you are a *Banause*!"

VIXEN — Female fox terrier and companion of Rudyard Kipling (1865 – 1936), Indian-born, patriotically British writer of stories and verse. His *Just So* animal stories are children's classics, and his *Jungle Book* has been immortalized by Disney.

Kipling, who had family connections with (once) famous creative Victorians, was addicted to dogs. In his poem "The Power of the Dog," he wrote,

> *Brothers and Sisters, I bid you beware*
> *Of giving your heart to a dog to tear.*

But of course he is most remembered for his stately verses, as in the final lines of "The Ballad of East and West":

> *But there is neither East nor West, Border nor Breed nor Birth,*
> *When two strong men stand face to face, though they come from the ends of the earth.*

He also managed to sound politically incorrect in his much quoted, "A woman is only a woman / But a good cigar is a smoke."

"Garm as Hostage," a relatively obscure but marvellous story in his voluminous works, centres on an emotional quadrangle — two dogs and two young men; Vixen is the sole female.

British colonialists in India kept many dogs, and these lived better than many of the "natives" and the wild pariah dogs. Into the happy life shared by Vixen and young Rudyard Kipling, then working as a journalist, comes Garm, unwished for and unhappily. Garm is an unbelievably intelligent bull terrier.

It all begins one evening as Kipling is on his way to the theatre.

In the middle of the road he sees a friend, an enlisted man named Stanley, dead drunk, shouting, making an awful scene. He takes the man home, puts him to bed, cleans him up the next morning, and returns him safely to the barracks.

Three days later Stanley appears at Kipling's house "with the most beautiful bull terrier I had ever seen." He had admired the dog at a distance for some time. "Vixen knew him too, but cared less for him."

Stanley explains that in thanks for Kipling's great help in rescuing him from that unfortunate episode, he is giving him his "most priceless possession." He is the best dog he has ever known, and besides, he is the "creation" of Stanley. "Please don't overfeed him, and don't try to give him back to him. And I won't tell you his name." Then Stanley runs the bull terrier through a series of admirable tricks — "Eyes right! Eyes left! Now die, but first dig your grave and then close your little eyes." The dog lies in the hole he has dug . . . "Now rise from the dead!"

Stanley gives Kipling a note saying once again not to try to return the dog, to name him whatever he cares to; that he can easily kill a man; not to give him too much meat. "He is more intelligent than a human."

Then Stanley runs off. His dog remains, howling miserably. Vixen bites him. "If Vixen were a male, he would have finished my dog," but as it was the new dog paid no attention to the little female "but put his head on my knee and tried to repress his wails."

Kipling writes that an ordinary street dog may be a flea-infested quadruped "considered unclean by Moses and Mohammed." But a dog that shares your home, a free creature that attaches itself to you full of love, that will not move without you, "a patient, quiet little soul that understands your mood before you do" — such a dog is in no way an ordinary dog.

That first evening Kipling had been planning to go to his club. But he could not leave the unhappy new dog, slinking and snuffling miserably through the house. So the three of them ate together — Vixen on one side of the writer, the strange dog on the other. Vixen watched every bite he took "and made it clear what she thought of his manners, which were actually much better than hers."

Vixen had always slept in bed with her master (who did not marry until several years later), and she had the endearing habit of trying to push him off the bed. Kipling describes in detail their first night *à trois*: Garm breathing miserably on the mat below the bed, Vixen viewing him from above with pure hatred, Kipling trying to pet Garm consolingly from the bed, Vixen on the verge of biting his other hand.

The story details the adventures, emotional and otherwise, of this triangular relationship during their months together, with attempted dog-nappings, heroic fights by Garm against attackers, his supremely intelligent good manners, and his increasing misery.

As summer approaches Garm becomes ill. He hardly eats, sleeps fitfully, dreams dramatic dreams. He grows thinner and

thinner. "He will die soon," they say in the officers' club. Kipling takes him to the top veterinarians and to a woman doctor, and recounts the strange story. Garm lies on the sofa and licks his hand.

"He is dying of a broken heart," says the woman doctor.

The veterinarian: "On my word, I believe she is right."

Garm gets some medicine, which helps briefly. Then Kipling learns that Stanley, too, has been very ill and has been sent to an army recuperation centre in the hills. The three of them, Garm, Kipling and Vixen, take the train and go to the centre.

When he once again meets Stanley, Kipling writes, "I thought that I had never in my life seen anything as miserable, bereaved, collapsed, as this little man leaning on the wall . . ."

The reunion between Stanley and Garm is a miraculous contrast. Garm suddenly "flies away" from Kipling, his legs barely seeming to move:

I heard the howls as he sprang up against Stanley and threw the little man to the ground. They rolled together on the earth, screaming, loving. I couldn't tell one from the other until Stanley finally stood up, whimpering.

They all go to a tea-house, and Stanley, for the first time in months, finally eats his fill — "that is, when Garm gave him a chance."

Garm understood the situation completely. He said goodbye to me three times, gave me both his paws, jumped on my shoulder for the last time. He ran along with us for about a mile (on the way to the station), singing Hosannas all the while. And then he raced back to his master.

Vixen did not say a word about all this. On the train ride back, she snuggled happily in Kipling's big coat. After being buttoned up inside, she gave a satisfied sigh and went to sleep on the writer's chest.

The final line of this great tear-jerker, written by a man's man, macho colonialist, is: "And on that evening, we were four of the happiest creatures on this earth."

WESSIE — Shaggy sheep dog, companion of Thomas Hardy (1840 – 1928), once widely-read Victorian novelist, lyricist, and dramatist. Wessie was obviously named after "Wessex" — once a kingdom of the West Saxons, and later widely familiar to Victorian readers because the name was used by Hardy to designate the counties, principally Dorset, where his novels take place — *Jude the Obscure, Tess of the d'Urbervilles, The Return of the Native*, and others.

Fifty years ago, a standard college textbook on English literature bore the title *From Beowulf to Thomas Hardy* — the names marking the first and last of anything worth studying. Since then, biographies have proliferated amazingly: the latest, an 868-page (yes) work entitled simply *Hardy*, takes violent issue with other recent biographies.

Pessimist, atheist, degenerate, realist — all these terms have been applied to Wessie's friend Hardy; he has also been said to "appear as a novelist in his poems, and as a poet in his novels," which "echo themes of Greek dramas" with their "tragic disappointments of life and love," and "with irony, and a bit of humour." No wonder Hardy liked the company of dogs.

Hardy and sex? In his Victorian day, he was condemned as a "decadent for dwelling on foul details" and with comments such as this, from the *National Review*:

> There are passages in *Jude* (published in 1896) which will offend men in direct proportion to their manliness, and which all women save the utterly abandoned will hurry over with shuddering disapproval.

But by his later years Hardy had become a venerated sage. Visitors, including celebrities, streamed to his village home, "Max

Gate." The first to announce company was Wessie, barking; then came discussions about literature, and walks — with Wessie — to show visitors the still-pastoral beauties of his village.

On one such occasion Hardy and a visitor walked to the small beautiful church in the village. At the grave "of a lady whose portrait was there on a medallion," Hardy's comment was: "She had many lovers."

Before entering the church, Hardy of course had to tie Wessie to a post outside. His comment here: "No doubt the dog is as good as many who go in."

A similar underlying Hardy view on churches and churchyards

may be found in this small piece of light verse, "The Levelled Churchyard":

Here's not a modest maiden elf
But dreads the final Trumpet,
Lest half of her should rise herself,
And half some local strumpet!

From restorations of Thy fane,
From smoothings of Thy sward,
From zealous Churchmen's pick and plane,
Deliver us, O Lord! AMEN!

What's a "fane"? Why, it's Middle English for "temple," as everybody who once read, once knew. Then what's a "sward"? Old English (from the Teutonic) for "grass lawn." Sixty years ago, there was still thought to be no question about Hardy's "ultimate popularity" — especially "the great epic-drama *The Dynasts*, the struggle of man against the force, neutral and indifferent to his sufferings, that rules the world."

Here it is our purpose to immortalize Wessie's character. We have evidence, from a conversation of 1922, documented by a literary visitor, that Hardy took seriously his observations about Wessie's animistic (or perhaps simply possessive) view of the world. With considerable pleasure, he explained to the visitor on this occasion that Wessie had two dishes. And these, according to Wessie, "evidently possessed feelings — for if anyone's foot touched them, up jumped the dog with a complaint."

From Hardy's voluminous writings, perhaps the appropriate one here would be from a collection titled *Afterwards*:

When the Present has latched its postern behind my tremulous
*   stay,*
And the May month flaps its glad green leaves like wings
Delicate-filmed as new-spun silk, will the neighbours say,
"He was a man who used to notice such things?"

"XANTI" — (Pronounced Zanti; name not historically verifiable). Devoted dog of Xanthippus (5th century B.C.), the father of Pericles.

Xanthippus was a member of a leading family of Athens during the period of the Persian Wars; under his famous son Pericles, Athens achieved her greatest heights as the centre of the world in art, literature, and architecture.

During the campaign of Thermopylae (*cf.* Lycas) in 480 B.C. between the Greeks and the Persians under Xerxes, the Greek fleet moved into the gulf between Athens and Salamis; the Persians destroyed Athens, whose citizens had fled to Salamis.

Against this background, Xanthippus' dog swam next to his master's galley all the way to Salamis. Pericles was about 15 years old at the time. His father's loyal dog was buried by his master on a promontory known ever since as Cynossema (Dog's Grave).

"ZODI" — Small dog almost always depicted together with Mithras, a mysterious cult figure worshipped in many localities of the Roman Empire. The god Mithras was depicted in cave paintings and statues busy killing a bull. As far as is known, this is the first time a name has been bestowed on his ancient but lively-looking dog. In astronomy, as will be seen, he is called Canis Minor.

The name "Zodi" (mnemonic, as the reader may by now have guessed) is a friendly abbreviation of "Zodiac," because the signs of the zodiac are an important part of the Mithraic mysteries. In sculptural and other contemporary representations of the killing of the bull — "tauroctony" as scholars call it — there are also always present, in addition to our feisty Zodi, a snake, a raven, and a scorpion. In astronomical terms, these represent Hydra, Corvus, and Scorpio, respectively, while the dog stands for Canis Minor, the "Lesser Dog Star."

For many years, scholars thought that the many bull-slaying scenes found throughout the Middle East and Europe in cave-like underground vaults and known as *mithraea*, must represent ideas taken from ancient Iranian mythology, because the name of the god worshipped in this cult, Mithras, is a Greek and Latin form of the name of an ancient Persian god.

However, a contemporary scholar is now convinced that the animals, sun, moon, stars, and other elements present in the *mithraeum* have nothing Iranian about them, but rather represent the almighty cosmic power of a unique deity, Mithras, who had "the power to move the entire universe, which he demonstrated by shifting the cosmic sphere in such a way that the spring equinox had moved out of Taurus the Bull" and into the sign of Aries.

Killing the bull, turning the cosmos. Zodi, right, helps.

The cult of Mithraism expanded throughout the Roman Empire at the same time as the new sect of Christianity. Hundreds of Mithraic temples have been discovered by archaeologists, and, it is now claimed, its many adherents included Roman soldiers stationed "abroad." Both Mithraism and its eventually triumphant rival Christianity, according to this theory, "shared an ideology of cosmic transcendence."

We cannot here explain the complex background of how the ancients viewed the cosmos, which is the key to the symbolism of this cult, and also to our Zodi. After all, an entire International Congress of Mithraic Studies was held in Manchester, England, in 1970.

"Canis Major," the "big dog" constellation, usually gets more attention than little "Canis Minor": he includes the brightest star, Sirius, whose "heliacal rising" ushered in the hot, dry season for ancient Greece: the "Dog Days."

There are more complications with inter-connecting Greek myths — for instance, the various stories about Hecuba, or Hecabe, and in her Cretan form, Hecate. She was the wife of Priam during the capture of Troy, and she was turned into a dog, and eventually a star. But it was fearless Zodi who always helped Mithras kill the bull — and turn the cosmos.